IN CHRIST I AM...

IN CHRIST I AM...

The Tween and Teen Guide to Knowing Who You Are in Christ

by
Janice Hylton-Thompson

Anointed Scribes Publishing
Newark NJ

Copyright © 2016 by Janice Hylton-Thompson

Unless otherwise noted Scripture taken from the New King James Version®. Copyright © 1982 by Thomas Nelson. Used by permission. All rights reserved.

Scriptures marked KJV are taken from the King James Version.

Scriptures marked AMP are taken from the Amplified® Bible, Copyright © 1954, 1958, 1962, 1964, 1965, 1987 by The Lockman Foundation

Used with permission." (www.Lockman.org)

Scriptures marked NLT are taken from the Holy Bible, New Living Translation, copyright 1996, 2004. Used with permission of Tyndale House Publishers, Inc., Wheaton, Illinois 60189. All rights reserved.

Scriptures marked NAS are taken from the New American Standard Bible®, Copyright © 1960, 1962, 1963, 1968, 1971, 1972, 1973, 1975, 1977, 1995 by The Lockman Foundation

Used with permission." (www.Lockman.org)

Scripture quotations marked (TLB) are taken from The Living Bible copyright © 1971. Used by permission of Tyndale House Publishers, Inc., Wheaton, IL 60189. All rights reserved.

IN CHRIST I AM...

ISBN-10: 1-946242-00-4

ISBN-13: 978-1-946242-00-6

P.O. Box 9881

Newark NJ 07104

All rights reserved.

No part of this book may be reproduced in any form without the written permission from the author, except for brief passages included in a review.

However, written permission not needed when quotations are used in church bulletins, orders of service, Sunday school lessons, church newsletters and similar works in the course of Christian instruction or services at a place of Christian worship or other Christian assembly.

Table of Contents

From My Heart to Yours	1
Introduction	3
To Parents and Guardians	5
To Youth and Teens	7
How To Be Born Again	11
How Will This Help Me?	13
Why Speak Good Things Over Your Life?	15
Others Favored by God	19
A Very Special Girl	21
God Promised to Bless You	25
Salvation	27
The New Me	51
God Loves Me	77
Benefits	93
Empowered	105

Thank You

Newark School of The Arts

I am so thankful that you do not turn away children with special needs, but instead welcome them with open arms, accept them, and give them an opportunity to learn like other children. I pray that the Lord will bless you tremendously, and may you continue to teach all children for years to come.

Mr. Price

Thank you for the anointing God has given you to teach children how to play instruments. Thank you especially for your patience and gifting, and the grace to teach Alexia how to play the drums.

Also, thank you so much for coming to our home to set up Alexia's drum set.

Other Staff

A very big thank you to the other staff who have taught her other classes. Your grace and gifting have helped Alexia to become the lover of music that she is today. Thank You!

Dedication

I dedicate this book to my very beautiful daughter Alexia who is blessed, gifted, anointed and appointed by God, for such a time as this!!

Alexia, you are my heartbeat, the smile on my face, the soft sounds of the raindrops on my roof that I can still hear when I was a little girl.

You, Alexia, are my passion and my drive, my fuel to keep me going and going and going.

You are my reminder that what God promises shall come to pass. You are the reason I rise every morning to pursue, possess and profess!

I love you very much my darling daughter, and I am so very proud of you and all that you have accomplished and all that God is doing in your life!

The Best Is Yet To Come!!

Love You To Life

Mom

From My Heart to Yours

I am the parent of a child with special needs. I was sixteen years old when I had my daughter, and basically raised myself and her. I discovered very early on that Alexia learned differently than other children. I wanted the best for her, and I was determined to get her every kind of help that I could possibly get her, so she could live a fulfilling life.

We have had a lot of challenges over the years, and I have had a lot of challenges personally with my own walk and faith in Christ. But in spite of it all, both Alexia and I know that we can do all things through Christ who strengthens us.

Regardless of the challenges, I wanted my daughter, affectionately known as "Lexi," to know who she is in Christ. At the publication of this book, my son Michael is twenty months. It is my desire that, from an early age, he begins to learn who he is in Christ.

I want my children, and all children and youth, to know that In Christ - you are saved, great, gifted, and anointed, and you are called by God to accomplish something great in life.

Know that you are called by God for such a time as this. God has great things in store for you. His plans are to bless you and prosper you in all that you do and to give you an expected end. What are you expecting from God? You cannot be expecting for God to do great things in your life if you do not know who you are in Christ.

If you do not know that God wants you to be saved, then you might live your whole life for the devil. If you do not know that God wants you to be blessed and prosperous, then you might just accept a mediocre life.

If you do not know that God wants you to have peace, you might live a life of turmoil and distress. If you do not know that God loves you, you might live a life thinking that God does not love you.

What is your name? The way you know your name and can say it without thinking is the same way God desires for you to know who you are in Christ. As you embark on this journey of learning who you are in Christ, may you receive all that He has for you, and may your life begin to transform into the young man or young lady that God created you to be.

In Christ I Am...

Introduction

In Christ I Am ... is a book that aims to empower you to know who you are in Christ, regardless of your age. While this book was written specifically for youth, even adults can read and learn from it because it is never too early or too late to learn about your new identity in Christ. This knowledge is found throughout the Bible from Genesis to Revelation. In knowing this, you will then be able to speak well of yourself by confessing God's Word over your life. Why? Because, according to Proverbs 18:21, **death and life is in the power of your tongue**. In other words, you will have what you say! By speaking the blessings of God's Word over your life, you will enjoy a happier and more joyous walk with the Lord Jesus Christ.

When I was growing up, I had heard a saying: "If you do not know who you are, you will answer to anything." That is precisely why knowing who you are in Christ is very important, because if you do not know, then you will answer to anything. The enemy does not want you to have this knowledge, because once you have it, you will speak with power and authority.

In some churches, we are taught not to speak well of ourselves. This has resulted in our children singing worldly songs where they sing words of condemnation and where they sing words of condemnation, labeling themselves things like 'sinners' and 'broken,' even though those words describe who they used to be, not who they are in Christ.

We are living in a time where 'good is bad' and 'bad is good'. There was a time that the word 'bad' meant 'bad', but today, 'bad means good'. These are the kinds of pressures and forces that our youth have to deal with on a daily basis. They hear such negative speech on television, radio, in school among their peers, etc.

Do not depend on the world to tell you who you are. Instead, learn what the Bible says about you. Learn to call yourself blessed, favored, and anointed, in accordance with God's Word. Such words and confessions command a blessing and not a curse on your lives. So go ahead and speak what the Lord says about you!

In Christ I Am...

To Parents and Guardians

As the Body of Christ, we are living in the last days according to the scriptures. Many scriptures are being fulfilled, and according to **2 Thessalonians 2:3**, there will be a great falling away of those who used to believe. The enemy is busy, and he is determined to get as many souls as possible to go to hell with him. **Psalms 127:3** declares that **"Children are a gift from God; they are his reward."** In spite of this, the enemy desires to take our gifts that God has given us to use for his purpose.

God, however, gave us our children for us to train them up in the fear and admonition of Him. God the Father desires to use them for His glory and honor, and for the advancement of His kingdom. It is therefore imperative, for us as parents, to help our children to understand who they are in God. God has a calling upon their lives, and He has good plans in store for them. God the Father's destiny and will for our children is that they invite Him to come into their lives, and to serve Him all of the days of their lives.

With this book, *In Christ I Am...*, my prayer is that our children will learn and apply who they are in the Lord Jesus Christ. I pray that they will walk in the power and authority that is in Him for their entire lives. I pray that God's perfect will for their lives will come to pass, and that they will experience the good plans that God has in store for them.

In Christ I Am...

To Youth and Teens

You are the most blessed, gifted, anointed, and awesome people that God has ever created! You are beautiful, wonderful, favored, and loved by God. You may not be the latest pop stars or superstars, but you are you! You were created in God's image to be used for His glory and honor. It is more important for you to know who you are in Christ than it is for you to know everything about those in Hollywood.

They have absolutely nothing on you! You have been anointed and appointed by God Himself for such a time as these last and final days. You are the next great thing! You are precious in the sight of God! You are loved by God so much that He sent His precious Son, Jesus Christ, to die for your sins.

God has great things in store for you. God wants you to walk in His will and destiny for your life that He planned before you were born. Jeremiah, who was a teen prophet, was called by God. In **Jeremiah 1:5**, God tells Jeremiah, **"Before I formed you in the womb I knew you; before you were born I sanctified you; I ordained you a prophet to the nations."**

The same goes for you today! Before God put you in your mother's belly, He knew you and had a plan for your life. He sanctified you and ordained you as a mouthpiece for His Kingdom. Sanctified means 'to set apart, to be set aside, to be picked out before.' In **Jeremiah 29:11**, the Lord tells Jeremiah, **"For I know the plans I have for you, says the Lord. They are plans for good and not for evil, to give you a future and a hope."** {TLB}

You Have a Savior Who Loves You and an Enemy Who Hates You

I would like to point out two important truths here. First, you have a Savior, the Lord Jesus Christ, who loves you unconditionally. Jesus loves you in spite of yourself, and there is nothing you can do to make Him stop loving you! Jesus loves you with an everlasting love, and He has good plans for you. That is why He left heaven and came to earth to die for you so that you can have eternal life.

The second truth is that you have an enemy – the devil, or Satan, who hates you unconditionally. The devil despises you! He hates you because

God loves you, and because you remind Satan of who he could have been. Long ago, Satan rejected God's plan for his life, suffered the consequences, and has been miserable ever since. That's the reason he wants us all to be miserable as he is. Your enemy has bad plans for your life, and works to destroy your life every chance he gets. Jesus says in **John 10:10, "The thief does not come except to steal, and to kill, and to destroy. I have come that they may have life, and that they may have it more abundantly."** To repeat, the enemy comes to STEAL, KILL, and DESTROY. Jesus, however, came so that you can have life and have it more abundantly. Jesus wants you to have a good, blessed, successful, safe, and abundant life.

Your Enemy Wants To Kill You

Let us take a closer look at the plans of the enemy, which are to <u>STEAL</u>, <u>KILL</u>, and <u>DESTROY</u>. Just think of the recent school shootings where innocent children were killed. Those incidents were all plans of the enemy. We also see many children and teens being killed by drugs, guns, gangs, and underage drinking, etc. Those are the plans of the enemy because he hates you.

And why does he hate you? He hates you because God loves you, and anything that God loves, the enemy hates. He hates you because God loves you so much that God himself died for you just to win you back from sin! I encourage you not to play with the enemy or his devices because he only wants to kill you.

Not only does the enemy want to kill you physically, but he also wants to keep you spiritually dead. When Adam sinned, all of us sinned in him, and became spiritually dead: we are selfish and rebellious by nature, ignoring and rejecting God's plan for our lives, unable to do the good things we want to do. Only accepting Jesus Christ as the Lord of our lives will bring us back to spiritual life.

The enemy has even convinced some children to commit suicide. Can you imagine feeling so hopeless that you want to end your own life? As we'll learn in this book, God loves you, and He put you on the earth at this time for a reason. His plans for you are great and wonderful, but the enemy wants to discourage you, to convince you that things are bad and will never get better. That's why this book is so important: we have to learn to recognize the enemy's lies, and we have to understand who we are in Christ so we can fight back against the lies.

Your Enemy Wants to Steal from You

If the enemy is not able to <u>KILL</u> you, then he will try to <u>STEAL</u> anything from you, including your peace and joy. He will send bullies into your path because you believe in Jesus Christ. He will send peer pressure to try and force you into using drugs, joining gangs, or having sex at an early age.

Having sex at an early age can lead to STDs (Sexually Transmitted Diseases). It can also lead to you becoming a teen parent, which is what happened to me. Sex outside of marriage as a teen can also lead to what is called 'soul-ties'. Your soul consists of your will, your intellect, and your emotions. To be 'soul-tied' is when you are so much into the person you had sex with that all you can do is think about them. This will cause you to do anything to please them. When your whole identity is tied up in another person, it's hard to live for God, so you can end up on missing out on his blessings. That's exactly what the enemy wants.

The enemy has also stolen the innocence of a lot of children by causing them to be raped, molested, or fondled by family members, friends, and others that they trust. Molestation was something I had to deal with at an early age because I was molested by close family members. If this is going on with you, please find someone you trust and tell them. You can tell a teacher, a guidance counselor, or someone else with whom you can feel safe.

Your Enemy Wants to Destroy You

If the enemy is not able to <u>KILL</u> you or <u>STEAL</u> from you, then he will try to <u>DESTROY</u> you. He has destroyed many young people's lives with drugs, underage drinking, gang violence, premarital sex, and so on. Many teens are in prison today because of crimes they have committed. Some will spend the rest of their lives in prison for those crimes, while others will be behind bars for a long time. That was all a plan of the enemy, since he will try to destroy young people's good names because of wrong choices they made.

Despite all the plans and intentions of the enemy, Jesus also pointed out in **John 10:10 "... I have come that they may have life, and that they may have it more abundantly."** Abundance means an overflow, having more than enough, and it starts with being born again.

In Christ I Am...
Why Must You Be Born Again?

You must be born again because Jesus paid the price to bring you back into a relationship with God the Father. His desire is that you will ask Him to come into your heart to live with you forever. It is not enough to grow up in the church if you have not asked Jesus to come into your heart. You must be born again!

John 3:16 states **"For God so loved the world that He gave his only begotten son that whosoever believes in him should not perish but have everlasting life."** Here you see that God loves you, and because of that love, He gave Jesus Christ, His Son, to die for you.

When Adam sinned in the Garden of Eden, something terrible happened to humanity. Instead of being born into an effortless relationship with God as Adam was, now we're born selfish and rebellious. We ignore God and the other authority figures in our lives, and we do whatever we want to even if we know it's wrong. That's why the Bible says we are lost before we come to know Jesus as our Savior.

There's great news, though. Just as we all fell into sin because of Adam's sin, we can also become righteous because Jesus died for our sins. The only thing we must do to receive Jesus' righteousness is to make Him the Lord of our lives. Christ forgave us when He died, even though we did not do anything to deserve His forgiveness.

There's a story in **John 3** about a man named Nicodemus. He came to Jesus by night because he was afraid of letting anyone see him. When Nicodemus went to Jesus to question Him, Jesus said to him, "You must be born again." Nicodemus asked Jesus how could he go back into his mother's belly and be born again. Jesus went on to explain to him that being born again does not mean for him to go back into his mother's belly. Nicodemus needed to be born of water and of Spirit. All of us were already born of water, which means to be born as a baby to our parents. The second birth, being born again, means that you need to be born in the Spirit, by accepting Jesus as Lord of your life.

How To Be Born Again

Let's look again at **John 3:16**, which says, **"For God so loved the world that he gave His only son, that whoever BELIEVES in Him should not perish but have ever lasting life."** Being born again, or saved, begins with believing in Jesus Christ. Another verse that will give you more understanding is **Romans 10:9**, which says, **"That if you confess with your mouth the Lord Jesus and believe in your heart that God has raised Him from the dead, you will be saved."** Another verse that goes hand in hand with the previous verse is **Revelation 3:20**, which states, **"Behold, I stand at the door and knock. If anyone hears my voice and opens the door, I will come in to him and dine with him, and he with me."**

When you confess to Jesus Christ and believe in your heart that God raised Him from the dead, then you are saved. If you've never done that, please do it now. Invite Jesus into your heart to live with you.

Prayer to Be Born Again

Pray the following with me: "I confess with my mouth to the Lord Jesus Christ, and I believe in my heart that God raised Him from the dead. Lord Jesus, I invite you to come into my heart and live with me." Congratulations! You are born again!

Now That I Am Born Again, What Next?

According to the Scriptures, you are now saved! It really is that easy to receive Jesus Christ into your heart as the Lord of your life. When you are born again, you are a new baby in God. Do you remember when you were a baby and your parents fed you the right food to help you grow healthy? The food you ate helped you grow and ensured that you would not die of hunger. It is the same way when you are a baby in Christ. As a born-again baby, you feed on Christ food, which is God's Word—the B.I.B.L.E.

You must think of the Bible as your favorite food. Wouldn't you like to eat your favorite food every day? In a way, the Bible is also a food that you need to eat every day.

The Bible is a big book! It has sixty-six smaller books in it, which are divided into two parts. The first part is the Old Testament, and the second part is the New Testament. It is a lot for you to read at one time, and it can be difficult to know where to begin.

I encourage you to do your best and read something every day. But let me make some suggestions for you. I have four recommendations on where you could begin:

1. You could begin in the **Book of Ephesians** because it tells you who you are in Jesus.

2. You could also begin in the **Gospels of Matthew, Mark, Luke and John**. The Gospels will help you get acquainted with your new Lord and Savior, Jesus Christ.

3. You can also begin with the **Book of John** because it talks about Christ's Lordship, and how he could be God and man at the same time. It will help you to get to know the Lord more intimately.

4. Finally, you could choose a certain topic and see what the Bible says about it. This book is an excellent example of studying the Bible in that kind of topical way. We're talking about the topic of "Who I am in Christ," and we're looking at all the Bible verses that touch on that theme.

How Will This Help Me?

In Christ I Am... will help you learn your identity in Christ. Now that you are a new baby in Christ, who are you really? If you do not know who you are, then you will believe you are whatever the enemy tells you that you are. When you know who you are in Christ, you will live a better life. You will be stronger in your walk with Christ and you will not believe the lies of the enemy.

This will help you in several ways in your day-to-day life.

- When you are faced with bullying and others are being mean, you need to know who you are in Christ.

- When you are being called names, you will not accept it because you will know who you are in Christ.

- When you are faced with peer pressure to drink, smoke, take drugs, join a gang, or have sex, you will know that God has better plans for you.

- When you are on the Internet, and you are tempted to look at pornography, the Holy Spirit will remind you that is not God's will for you. You will know that you are too precious and special to God to look at things that do not please Him. You will see that it is all about knowing who you are and the power that lives within you.

- When you are sad about something or have lost a loved one, and the enemy whispers lies and suicidal thoughts to you, you will remember that God loves you and He has a plan for you. If the enemy wants you to take your life, you will know that God died to give you life and that you are precious. God wants you to live, but the enemy wants you to die at a young age. He does not want you to live your life for God, and honor Him with it.

Why Is It Important to Say or Confess God's Word?

Proverbs 18:21, states **"Death and life *are* in the power of the tongue, and those who love it will eat its fruit."** In other words, you will have what you say. So if you say you are stupid, then guess what? You will be stupid! If you say you are smart, then guess what? You will be smart! If you say you are sick, then you will be sick. But if you say that you are healed, then you will be healed.

Does that mean if you feel sick in your body you should not go to the doctor or tell your parents? Of course not! What it means is that even though you might not feel well in your body, you should speak God's Word of healing over your body instead of speaking words of sickness.

When you have a test in school, do not say, "I won't do well. I'm going to fail!" Instead, say "I will do well. I will pass this test!" In moments like these, bring **Deuteronomy 28:13** to mind, and confess, **"I am the head and not the tail. I shall be only above and not beneath."**

God and His angels are waiting to hear what you have to say so that they can move on your behalf. Not only are God and His angels waiting to hear what you have to say, but also the enemy and his fallen angels are waiting for the same. If you let negative words come out of your mouth, they will use those negative words against you. Whatever is in your heart comes out in your words. This is why it is important to learn God's Word so that it can be in your heart!

In this book, In Christ I Am..., you will learn who God says you are. You will get God's Word in your heart so that you can speak it over your life, which will help you live a victorious and fulfilling Christian life.

Why Speak Good Things Over Your Life?

Some people think it's a bad thing for you to speak well of yourself. However, God speaks good things over us all the time, and the Bible is full of good things for us to say about ourselves. God wants us to speak His Word over our lives because His Word is good and full of blessings and promises. When you speak God's Word over your life, you speak it always, every day, in every situation. God has spoken well of a number of the children in the Bible. Others have spoken well of themselves. The following are some examples of people who spoke good things over their lives.

Abraham: A Friend of God

Abraham, the father of the Jews, is known as a friend of God. You can read this in **James 2:23**, which states, **"And the Scripture was fulfilled which says, 'Abraham believed God, and it was accounted to him for righteousness.' And he was called the friend of God."** Not only was Abraham a friend of God, but he also became the father of the Jewish nation, and in him, God promised that the Savior, Jesus Christ, would come through his bloodline.

Moses: the Meekest Man

Numbers 12:3 states, **"Now the man Moses was very meek, above all the men which were upon the face of the earth."**

This verse is a perfect example of speaking good things over your life. Moses was inspired by God to write the first five books of the Bible. Moses wrote that he was the meekest man, which meant that he was humble and patient. Like Moses, speak those things that you desire to see come to pass in your life. Even when you don't feel humble or patient, speak it anyway, and watch what God does!

Joseph: Was Loved More than His Siblings

Joseph is my favorite person in the Bible because his life is a perfect example of a believer's life – full of tests, trials, and triumphs. **Genesis 37:3** says, **"Now Israel loved Joseph more than all his children, because he** *was* the son of his old age. Also, he made him a tunic of *many* colors." Not only did Jacob love Joseph more than he loved the rest of his children, but he also favored him with a beautiful coat of many colors. Joseph is a picture or example of Jesus, and his coat represented authority and the nations of the world that would come to Jesus.

Joshua: Chosen by God

You will first meet Joshua in **Exodus 17**, where he fights against the Amalekites, a people who did not like the Israelites. As you follow the life of Joshua, you will see that he becomes Moses' assistant, and persistently follows in Moses' footsteps. Joshua is most famously known for being one of the two spies who brought back a good report about the Promised Land to Moses and the people. It was no wonder that when Moses died, God chose Joshua to lead His people into the Promised Land. You can read more about Joshua in the book that is named after him.

Ruth: Great-Grandmother of King David

Ruth is one of my favorite women in the Bible, if not my absolute favorite. She is a young woman who was a Moabite, meaning she wasn't originally one of God's people, but she was married to an Israelite named Mahlon. Mahlon's family came to live in Moab after they had left Bethlehem-Judah. After some time, Mahlon, his father, and his brother were killed in battle. Ruth then went back to Bethlehem with her mother-in-law, Naomi. There, she ended up marrying Boaz, an extremely wealthy family member of Naomi's. Ruth and Boaz had a son whose name was Obed, and who was the father of Jesse, the father of David, the father of King Solomon. This was the bloodline that Jesus our Savior came through.

Esther: The Young Queen

Esther's story is one of my very favorites. In fact, there is a whole book in the Bible named after her, and that's where you can find her story. While the Bible doesn't say how old Esther was, it does describe her as young, lovely, and beautiful. She was raised by Mordecai, her cousin, who took her as his own daughter because her parents had died and because she was the daughter of his uncle. As time goes on, the King was in need of a new queen, and Esther was chosen to be the queen.

Janice Hylton-Thompson

David: Chosen by God as a Child

It's fascinating to read the story of how God chose David to be king. When you have time, please read about David in **2 Samuel**. David was the youngest of his brothers. When Israel needed a new king, the Lord sent the prophet Samuel to the house of Jesse, David's father. The prophet thought that God had chosen one of David's six brothers, but God did not choose them. Finally, Samuel asked if Jesse had any other children. Jesse said he had a younger son who was keeping the sheep. Samuel told Jesse to send for him and bring him to the house. When David arrived, God told Samuel that David was the one who would be king over Israel, and for Samuel to anoint him.

Daniel, Shadrach, Meshach, Abednego:
Chosen by the King

The four Hebrew boys — Daniel, Shadrach, Meshach, and Abednego — were chosen by the king. You can find their story in the **Book of Daniel**. In **Daniel 1:4** they were described as **"young men in whom *there was* no blemish, but good-looking, gifted in all wisdom, possessing knowledge and quick to understand, who *had* ability to serve in the king's palace, and whom they might teach the language and literature of the Chaldeans."** They had to go through a time of purification, after which they were found to be ten times wiser than all the wise men. The king was so pleased with them that he put them in leadership positions.

Even though the King favored them, there were others who hated them. King Nebuchadnezzar made an image of gold and ordered everyone to bow to it. However, the Hebrew boys only worshipped and bowed down to the God of Abraham. The King had decreed that whoever would not bow to the statue and worship it would be cast in the firey furnace.

Well, the Hebrew boys refused, and those who were jealous of them went and told the King that they refused to worship the statue. The King decided to give them another chance to bow and worship the statue. Once again, the Hebrew boys refused, and said they would worship no one but the true God. The King had his men to throw the boys in the fiery furnace. The fire was so hot that the men who threw the boys in the fire died.

Guess what happened? Even though the boys were in the fire, God did not allow it to hurt them, and as a matter of fact, there was a fourth person in the fire. In **Daniel 3:25** it states, **"Look!"** he answered, **"I see four** men loose, walking in the midst of the fire; and they are not hurt, and the form of the fourth is like the Son of God." Wow!!! Isn't this an awesome story?

The lesson is in this story is that when your faith is tested, depend on Christ to see you through. Even when these boys' lives were in danger, they refused to sin against God, and He came to their aid, just as He will always come to yours. The story of these three Hebrew boys is one of peer pressure and bullying. Others will try to bully you into doing the wrong thing, because the devil's desire is to kill you, steal your joy, or destroy you however he can. Remember, though, that Christ wants you to depend on him regardless of what they want you to do. Others will try to pressure you into doing what they want you to do but please try to remember this story and do the right thing!

Others Favored by God

The list of young people, teens, tweens, and children who God has used for His glory goes on and on. There is Samuel, whom God spoke to when he was young. Josiah was anointed king when he was eight. In the New Testament, John the Baptist was chosen as the forerunner of Jesus Christ, which meant he was the person who came before Jesus Christ to prepare the way for him. Jesus said that John the Baptist was the greatest prophet that had ever lived.

Then there is the other John, repeatedly described in the Bible as "the one whom Jesus loved." He was one of the twelve disciples handpicked by Jesus, and was one of the three disciples that Jesus shared his most intimate moments with, such as when Jesus went to meet Moses and Elijah on the mount and when Jesus was praying in the garden. If I asked you to picture Jesus' disciples, you would probably imagine older men. But did you know that John may have been as young as twelve years old when he was chosen to be a disciple? That should tell you something about how much Jesus loves kids and teens!

This same John was also the one that Jesus trusted for the care of His mother when He was on the cross. An important thing to remember about John the beloved is that he wrote the book of John, meaning he was the one who kept referring to himself as "the one whom Jesus loved." He wrote those words about himself. Do you truly think of yourself as "the one whom Jesus loves"? Do you speak those words over your life on a daily basis, or even repeatedly throughout the day? How would you feel if you were constantly being reminded of Jesus' love for you?

There was also Stephen, a young man who loved the Lord Jesus, and who is known as the first martyr, or the first person who was killed because he believed in Jesus. He is described as a man full of faith and of the Holy Spirit. You can read his story in **Acts 7**.

Then there is the story of Saul, who was a persecutor of the church. His name was later changed to Paul, and he was known as the Apostle Paul. On his way to hunt down and kill Christians in the city of Damascus, he was knocked off his horse and heard the voice of Jesus speaking directly to him. Saul became a great apostle who spread the Gospel of Jesus Christ to many people. He also wrote most of the New Testament. You can read his story beginning in **Acts 9**.

There is a young lady named Rhoda, who is rarely referred to. You can read her story in **Acts 12**. Peter, one of Jesus' disciples, was imprisoned by King Herod. Miraculously, Peter got out of prison when an angel of the Lord freed him. Peter went to the house where the saints were praying and knocked on the door. Rhoda answered the door as she recognized Peter's voice and told the others that Peter was at the door.

You see, it is not always about doing something big and great in your eyes for the kingdom of God. It could be something as simple as opening a door for the people of God.

Another young person I will mention here is Timothy, one of my favorite people in the Bible. Timothy's biological father was not Jewish, but Greek, and was not able to teach Timothy the things of the Lord. However, Timothy's mother and grandmother were Jewish, and taught Timothy the Holy Scriptures. Additionally, the person that had the most impact on Timothy was his spiritual father, the Apostle Paul, who led him to the Lord. I love this story because we see the Apostle Paul teaching young Timothy about the ministry as they traveled together. Along with teaching Timothy, Paul trained and prepared Timothy for the ministry. Eventually, Paul also sent Timothy to churches as he was preparing to become a young pastor himself. You can read more about Timothy in the two books that bear his name — **First Timothy** and **Second Timothy**.

As you can see from these examples, God used a lot of young people to help to accomplish his plans and destiny. In a similar manner as God used them and spoke well of them, He speaks well of you too and wants to use you. Are you ready to come along with Him?

A Very Special Girl

The final young person that I would like to mention but certainly not the least is the beautiful young lady on the cover of this book. My lovely daughter Alexia, or Lexi for short. I had Lexi when I was sixteen years old. At that age I should have been in school, enjoying my friends and being a teenager. But I disobeyed God's Word by fornicating, and I got pregnant. I chose to bring Lexi into this world. We faced a number of challenges — being homeless, suffering from sickness, etc.

I was seventeen years old, Alexia was one year old, and we were homeless. We went from house to house, sleeping on people's couches, floors, and wherever we could find a place. I remember one time when I picked up the phone to call Children Protective Services, thinking perhaps they could give us a foster home together. Then I thought about the fact that I would be eighteen years old soon and would no longer be a ward of the state, and I did not want the state to take my baby away from me. I ended up allowing Alexia to stay with family friends in New York so I could finish school in New Jersey, and I visited her on the weekends. It was so hard to be away from my baby! I didn't like the decisions I was forced to make, but I had put myself in that position through my own disobedience. After a few months, I went and got her because I just couldn't stand to be away from my baby, and it was best for us to stay together.

Thankfully, God, opened a home for us with a warm, loving, and supportive family, who were members of the church we attended. The Caddles and Betheas took us in and made us a part of their own family! Alexia faced a number of challenges as well. She was classified very early on as learning-disabled, but I was determined to get her all of the help she needed to live the best life possible. I got her into an early intervention program for kids with special needs, which was able to provide her with counseling and therapy.

Lexi and I were faithful members at church. She loved to sing in the choir and she loved Sunday school. When Lexi was four years old, she asked Jesus to come into her heart and save her. Not only did she receive Jesus, but one day she told me that God wants her to be a pastor. Can you imagine? A pastor?

A few memories stand out in my mind, but one in particular brings tears to my eyes every time I think of it. I remember one evening when I was kneeling at my bed praying and crying out to God for a number of issues we were facing. One in particular was Alexia being a special needs child. I was crying out to God for Him to manifest his healing power and heal Alexia totally. As I was praying and crying, Alexia came over to me and wiped my tears away. "Mommy, don't cry; it's going to be ok." Those little two-year-old hands wiping my tears made me cry harder. I shared this story because it's not always something 'big' that God will use you to get your attention and speak to you. He might speak through a passionate preacher, or He might speak through a toddler. You can hear His voice anywhere once you know how He speaks, which we'll learn in the next section of this book.

Over the years, we have faced many more challenges, but in the midst of it all, I remind her who God has called her to be. I remind her of who she is in Christ. I pray over and for her daily. I speak God's Word to and into her life daily. As Lexi grew, I taught her how to speak God's Word over her life. I taught her how to go to the Lord in prayer for herself and for her to expect what she's praying for.

Again, the beautiful young lady on the cover playing the drums is my precious daughter Alexia, who is now a young adult. Let me share her story about the drum set. For years Alexia wanted a drum set because she loves music and especially loves the drums. She would pretend she was playing the drums by using pencils or whatever she could find, beating on cups, pots, containers, or even her bed. From time to time she would ask me to buy her a drum set, and I would tell her to pray that the Lord would bless her, because I try to use every opportunity to help her exercise her faith and get into her heart to pray about everything. In the meantime, I registered her to take lessons at The Newark School of Arts.

At this point we were living in a one-bedroom apartment; I gave her the bedroom and I slept in the living room. We didn't have the space to put a drum set or the finances to purchase one. Additionally, I was trying to save every extra penny I had because I was also working on purchasing our first home.

Nevertheless, I saved up enough money for a drum set, and I wanted to surprise her for her sixteenth birthday. When I bought the drum set, the box was so big it could hardly fit through the door. We opened the box, even though we didn't have any space to set it up. We took the two smaller drums out and put them on top of the box, and she would practice about an hour per day. Sometimes, she would take them in her room and practice.

A few years later, the Lord blessed us with our first home, and there was more than enough space for her drums, which Mr. Price, her drum lessons teacher, came and set up for us. Now, she has the whole drum kit, set up where she can play it without limitation.

You see, there's nothing you put your heart and mind to that you are not able to accomplish. When Alexia was about two and half, she was classified as special needs. I was told by the child study team, doctors, and specialist, that there were things she wouldn't be able to do. Well, I am here to tell you that Alexia has accomplished so much in her life. She only needed the opportunities so that she could apply herself. Alexia has overcome many challenges because together we trust the Lord that she can do all things through Christ that strengthens her.

It doesn't matter how big or small your dreams: I want to encourage you that you can overcome! You can accomplish whatever you put your heart and mind to. When Mr. Price set up Alexia's drum set, I remember saying "Wow, it is so big; it's even bigger than the one at the music school." But it doesn't matter how big your situation is. If you have what you need, you can overcome.

That is why I placed her on the cover of this book In Christ I Am..., because she was able to tackle this big drum set and make sweet music. So I encourage you today that you can do all things through Christ who strengthens you. Pray and ask God for what you need to overcome and he will give you what you need.

So I want to encourage you as you read this book. Growing up, you will face many challenges, but trust the Lord. Speak only what God has spoken over and about your life. You will be faced with many decisions, peer pressure, and circumstances that will challenge who you are. When you go to college, there will be efforts to get you to turn your back on what you were taught as a child, but remember who you are and whose you are. You are a child of the Most High God and King. You belong to Christ, because He shed his blood for you! You are loved by God and you are one of His representatives. You are God's child and you are loved by God!

In Christ I Am...

God Promised to Bless You

While God has delivered us from the curse of the law, He has not delivered us from the blessings of the law. What does that mean? The Old Testament is considered the law, even though God only gave 10 commandments. Some believe that since we are not under the "law" anymore, then there's no need for us to read the Old Testament. This, of course, is incorrect – there's never a good reason to start chopping parts out of the Bible! The Old Testament is our old schoolmaster or teacher, and the New Testament instructs us to read and learn from the many stories included in those books.

Many scriptures in the Old Testament continue blessing us even today. **Deuteronomy 28: 1-14** is beautiful, and contains God's promise to bless you. Please read it and think about how God said He would bless you and your family. He has promised to bless you in every area of your life including your health, your finances, those who dislike you, your traveling, and much more. So whenever things are not going right in any area of your life, remember that God has promised to bless you. Take authority or control of the situation by speaking the blessings of God over your life. In order to speak the blessings of God or His word over your life, it is important for you to know His Word. If you do not know His word, you will not be able to speak it over yourself. This book is an excellent first step in learning what God has to say about who you are in Him!

How to Use This Section

In this section, you will learn who you are in Christ. We will look at a few ways to help you to understand better who God says you are. Read one each day and meditate or think on that one verse for that day. Memorize the scripture and have it in your heart so that you can speak it back to yourself whenever you need to hear it again. You will also be able to write the verse down which will help you to memorize it more easily.

This section is divided into five smaller parts. You can read them all in order, or you can choose what you would like to study or spend more time learning about. When you accepted Jesus Christ into your life, everything about you changed, so let's learn how!

The sections include:

1. Salvation
2. The New Me
3. Love
4. Benefits
5. Empowered

Janice Hylton-Thompson

SALVATION

We All Sinned and Deserved Hell!

Adam sinned against God by disobeying Him; therefore, we all became sinners and we were all separated from God.

Genesis 2:15-17

[15]Then the Lord God took the man and put him in the garden of Eden to tend and keep it. [16]And the Lord God commanded the man, saying, "Of every tree of the garden you may freely eat; [17]but of the tree of the knowledge of good and evil you shall not eat, for in the day that you eat of it you shall surely die."

Genesis 3:4-7

[4]Then the serpent said to the woman, "You will not surely die. [5]For God knows that in the day you eat of it your eyes will be opened, and you will be like God, knowing good and evil."

[6]So when the woman saw that the tree was good for food, that it *was* pleasant to the eyes, and a tree desirable to make *one* wise, she took of its fruit and ate. She also gave to her husband with her, and he ate. [7]Then the eyes of both of them were opened, and they knew that they were naked; and they sewed fig leaves together and made themselves coverings.

But God Loved Us Too Much!

John 3:16

For God so loved the world that he gave his only begotten son, that whoever believes in him should not perish but have everlasting life.

You Must Be Born Again

1 Corinthians 15:20-22

[20]But now Christ is risen from the dead, and has become the first fruits of those who have fallen asleep. [21]For since by man *came* death, by Man also *came* the resurrection of the dead. [22]For as in Adam all die, even so in Christ all shall be made alive.

Example

I Am Created in God's Image

Genesis 1:27

So God created man in His own image; in the image of God He created him; male and female He created them.

Today, our verse will help you know that you were created in God's image. Do not try to look like your favorite pop star or the popular kid at school, because you can't live in God's perfect plan for your life if you're pretending to be someone else! Every day, remember that God created you in his own image. When you look in the mirror at yourself, you are looking into the eyes of God.

<u>Say it, Believe it, Think it, and Be it!</u>
I am created in God's image.

<u>Write Today's Promise</u>

So God Created man in his own image, in the image of God; He created him; male and female, He created them.

<u>Write Today's Confession</u>

I am created in the image of God.

<u>What Do You Think about Today's Promise?</u>

Janice Hylton-Thompson
I Am Crucified with Christ
Galatians 2:20

I am crucified with Christ: nevertheless I live; yet not I, but Christ lives in me: and the life which I now live in the flesh I live by the faith of the Son of God, who loved me, and gave himself for me.

When Christ died for you, He became sin for you. He took your place of punishment, and God put all of your sins, sickness, and disease upon and within Him. When Jesus took your place, you were also crucified with Him and your sins died with Him. Because of this, when you asked Jesus to come into your heart, He came to live inside you, and is alive in you today. Therefore, the life you are now living is Christ living in and through you. You now live by faith because Christ loves you and gave Himself for you.

<u>Say it, Believe it, Think it, and Be it!</u>
I am crucified with Christ, and Christ lives within me.

<u>Write Today's Promise</u>

_____

_____

<u>Write Today's Confession</u>

_____

_____

<u>What Do You Think about Today's Promise?</u>

_____

_____

In Christ I Am...

I Am Redeemed Through Christ's Blood

Ephesians 1:7

In Him we have redemption through His blood, the forgiveness of sins, according to the riches of His grace.

Today, you will learn two more powerful words. The first is 'redemption.' Redeem means 'to buy back'. When you sinned, you became property of the devil. Christ, however, paid the ultimate price for our sins, and bought us back for himself. In this verse, Paul wants you to know that you have redemption through the blood of Jesus Christ.

The other word is 'forgiveness,' which means 'to put away or dismiss.'

Everyone wants to be forgiven by people, but we especially want to be forgiven by God. We can only receive forgiveness from God through the blood of Jesus Christ, and we received that forgiveness the moment we asked him to be the Lord of our lives. No matter what you do or the mistakes you make, always remember that God has already forgiven you of your past, present and future sins and mistakes. Walk in the forgiveness of God, and do not allow anyone to take that away from you. Pray and ask your heavenly father to help you stop making those mistakes or missing the mark. He is always available to help you be more like Christ.

<u>Say it, Believe it, Think it, and Be it!</u>
I am redeemed and forgiven by God.

<u>Write Today's Promise</u>

_____

_____

<u>Write Today's Confession</u>

_____

_____

<u>What Do You Think about Today's Promise?</u>

_____

_____

Janice Hylton-Thompson

I Am Forgiven

1 John 2:12

I write to you, little children, because your sins are forgiven you for His name's sake.

'Forgiveness,' as you just learned, means to put away, dismiss or pardon. Forgiving others when they hurt you isn't always easy, even for those of us who have made Jesus the Lord of our lives. Notice how the Apostle John addressed you. He began by calling you 'little children'. You may remember reading in the Bible about how parents brought their little children to Jesus. He blessed and prayed for them because children are very special to the Lord. You are very special to God, too! He knows you by name and He knows everything about you!

The Apostle John wants you to know that your sins are forgiven for Christ's sake. It is for you to remember the following: Forgiveness is given and not earned! Forgiveness is not based on what you have done or how good you are, but forgiveness is based on Jesus' blood and righteousness. Forgiveness is always available, so do not ever allow yourself to feel condemned or guilty, because Jesus died so that you can be forgiven of your past, present, and future sins, faults and mistakes. Now, the same way Christ has forgiven you, it is His desire that you forgive others also. You are not forgiving someone because they deserve it, but you are forgiving someone for Christ's sake, and because Christ has forgiven you.

<u>Say it, Believe it, Think it, and Be It!</u>
I am forgiven because of Jesus.

<u>Write Today's Promise</u>

_____

_____

<u>Write Today's Confession</u>

_____

_____

<u>What Do You Think about Today's Promise?</u>

_____

_____

In Christ I Am...

I Am Saved

Romans 10:9

That if you confess with your mouth the Lord Jesus and believe in your heart that God has raised Him from the dead, you will be saved.

    This verse was mentioned earlier, and I would like to make it one of your daily verses. It states that if you will confess with your mouth the Lord Jesus, and believe in your heart that God raised him from the dead, you will be saved. It is just that simple. It has to do with what you say with your mouth and believe in your heart. If you have not already, go ahead and ask Jesus to come into your heart. Did you notice that the Apostle Paul did not say to confess your sins? He said to confess the Lord Jesus Christ! Confess or say that you believe He is the Son of God, who died for you and rose again. That is what separates us from what other religions believe about Jesus Christ. We don't just believe that he was a prophet or good teacher; we believe that He is the Son of God!

<u>Say it, Believe it, Think it, and Be It!</u>

I confess with my mouth the Lord Jesus Christ, and I believe in my heart that God raised Him from the dead, and now, I am saved.

<u>Write Today's Promise</u>

_____

_____

<u>Write Today's Confession</u>

_____

_____

<u>What Do You Think about Today's Promise?</u>

_____

_____

Janice Hylton-Thompson

I Am Saved by Grace

Ephesians 2:8-9

For by grace you have been saved through faith, and that not of yourselves; it is the gift of God: not of works, lest anyone should boast.

There is nothing anyone can do to be saved outside of Jesus Christ. We cannot be good enough; we cannot do enough good deeds, and we cannot pay enough money. Salvation comes by God's grace when we have faith and accept the price Jesus paid on the cross. Again, we are saved by grace, through faith. Grace means undeserved favor. We do not deserve God's grace, but he gives it freely because of His love for us. Faith is putting our trust in what Christ has done already for us. So, because Christ died for us, we put our faith and trust in His sacrificial death, so that we can be born again.

Salvation is a gift; it is nothing that we have done to be saved. It is not through works that we are saved, because salvation comes only through Jesus Christ and His death and resurrection.

<u>Say it, Believe it, Think it, and Be It!</u>
I am saved by grace through faith in Jesus Christ.

<u>Write Today's Promise</u>

_____

_____

<u>Write Today's Confession</u>

_____

_____

<u>What Do You Think about Today's Promise?</u>

_____

_____

In Christ I Am...

I Am Delivered

1 Thessalonians 5:23

And the very God of peace sanctify you wholly; and I pray God your whole spirit and soul and body be preserved blameless unto the coming of our Lord Jesus Christ.

We have to understand salvation before we can understand deliverance. Salvation doesn't just mean our souls are saved; that's only the starting point. Christ desires that our souls be delivered, but just as much, He also desires that every part of us be delivered.

We say that God is a Trinity, made up of God the Father, God the Son and God the Holy Spirit, just like you are one person made up of a body, a soul, and a spirit. We are a spirit that possesses a soul and lives in a body. When Jesus died, He didn't just die to save our souls from hell, but He died to save every part of us. He delivered or redeemed all of who we were before Adam sinned. The term 'delivered' is a word that goes hand in hand with salvation. We are delivered from everything that is not like God, whether that's sin, oppression, sickness, disease, poverty, or anything else that doesn't bring the abundant life Jesus talked about. We are fully restored, freed to live for Him.

God wants us saved, delivered, healed, in our right minds. God came to save and delivered all of who we are.

Say it, Believe it, Think it, and Be It!
I am delivered, and God's peace sanctifies me wholly!

Write Today's Promise

_____

_____

Write Today's Confession

_____

_____

What Do You Think about Today's Promise?

_____

_____

Janice Hylton-Thompson

I Am Born of God

1 John 5:18

We know that whoever is born of God does not sin; but he who has been born of God keeps himself, and the wicked one does not touch him.

As you grow in the Lord, you will make mistakes, which the Bible calls sinning. In spite of this, remember that you are born of God; you are born again. Jesus paid the price for your sins and mistakes! Regardless of your mistakes, God sees you through the blood of Christ and does not see you as a mess-up or a failure. When you sin, God does not see your sins; instead, He sees the blood and the love of Christ. God is your keeper, and He is the one who keeps you safe so the devil, your enemy, cannot touch you. While the enemy wants to destroy you, God wants to protect you! Dismiss the enemy's lies when he tries to talk about your failures, and speak God's freedom over your life, knowing that God is your keeper.

<u>Say it, Believe it, Think it, and Be It</u>
I am born of God, and I am kept by God.

<u>Write Today's Promise</u>

_____
_____

<u>Write Today's Confession</u>

_____
_____

<u>What Do You Think about Today's Promise?</u>

_____

In Christ I Am...
I Am a Gift from God

Psalm 127:3

**Behold, children are a heritage from the Lord,
the fruit of the womb is a reward.**

    This is one of my favorite scriptures about children. Children are gifts from the Lord, and the fruit of the womb is a reward, or is blessed. This means that when your mother carried you in her belly, you were blessed already, and you were a gift from God to your parents. You are so special to God that He gave you to your parents. You are a gift from God, and in turn, God desires that you will be a gift to Him by living your life for Him. Remember, you are not here by accident, and you are not a mistake. Even if your parents didn't plan you, God planned you. He created you on purpose, to be a blessing to others and to Him. Stand firm on that promise, and know you have great value.

<u>Say it, Believe it, Think it, and Be It!</u>
I am a gift from God, and I am blessed!

<u>Write Today's Promise</u>

_____

_____

<u>Write Today's Confession</u>

_____

_____

<u>What Do You Think about Today's Promise?</u>

_____

_____

Janice Hylton-Thompson

I Am Alive to God

Romans 6:10-11

For the death that He died, He died to sin once for all; but the life that He lives, He lives to God. Likewise you also, reckon yourselves to be dead indeed to sin, but alive to God in Christ Jesus our Lord.

When Christ died for you, He paid the price for all your sins of the past, present, and future. Christ died once for you and for everyone else. He will not have to get back upon the cross every time you sin or miss the mark. 'To reckon' means to think of yourself as dead to sin. Sin is no longer fun or desirable to you. But what kinds of sin are we talking about? We refer to anything that is not pleasing to God, your Father, as sinning or missing the mark. Have your parents ever promised you a reward for doing something, such as getting good grades or cleaning your room? If you don't do the thing they said, you don't get the reward. In the same way, you can't get God's biggest blessings unless you do the things He says to do, because His blessings come through obedience. Remind yourself you are dead to sin but are alive to God in Jesus, your Lord.

<u>Say it, Believe it, Think it, and Be It!</u>

I am alive to God

<u>Write Today's Promise</u>

_____

_____

<u>Write Today's Confession</u>

_____

_____

<u>What Do You Think about Today's Promise?</u>

_____

_____

In Christ I Am...

I Am Known by God

Jeremiah 1:5

Before I formed you in the womb I knew you; before you were born I sanctified you; I ordained you a prophet to the nations.

Our verse for today declares that you are known by God. God knew you before he put you in your mother's belly. Not only did He know you, but He sanctified you, which means He separated you and set you aside. God claimed you for Himself, so you could do His purpose and His will. He also ordained you, or anointed you, to share His word with everyone. If you are known to God, that means you are very special to Him.

<u>Say it, Believe it, Think it, and Be It!</u>

I am known by God!

<u>Write Today's Promise</u>

_____

_____

<u>Write Today's Confession</u>

_____

_____

<u>What Do You Think about Today's Promise?</u>

_____

_____

Janice Hylton-Thompson

I Am a Child of God

John 1:12

But as many as received Him, to them He gave the right to become children of God, to those who believe in His name.

Have you ever heard someone say that we are all children of God? Well, that is not correct according to the Bible. This verse clearly states that in order to be a child of God, you must receive Him. Have you received Jesus? Have you asked Jesus to come into your heart and life and live with you? If you have, then, congratulations, you are a child of God! It really is that simple. If you have not, please flip back a few pages to the section on "Why Must You Be Born Again?" Asking Jesus to come into your heart is the most important decision you will ever make. Take the time to ask Jesus to come into your heart! If you've already done it, remember that God is now your Father. He loves you and He is proud of you, and the thought of you brings Him great delight.

<u>Say it, Believe it, Think it, and Be It!</u>
I am a Child of God!

<u>Write Today's Promise</u>

_____

_____

<u>Write Today's Confession</u>

_____

_____

<u>What Do You Think about Today's Promise?</u>

_____

_____

In Christ I Am...
I Am Free from the Law
Romans 8:2

For the law of the Spirit of life in Christ Jesus has made me free from the law of sin and death.

"The law of the Spirit of Life in Christ Jesus" means living by faith. The law of the Spirit has set us free from the law of sin and death, which is also known as the Law of Moses. The Law of Moses is also called the Ten Commandments, and includes many other rules and regulations found in the first five books of the Bible. Only Jesus could perfectly obey the Law of Moses, thus fulfilling it and making us free from the law of sin and death. When Christ died and you accepted Him into your life, you were given credit for obeying the whole Law of Moses, freeing you from the law of sin and death.

Walk in your freedom in Christ because of the blood of Jesus. You see, the law of sin and death made us feel guilty and ashamed because it was created to help us to see that we could not keep it. We needed someone to keep it for us, and that was Jesus. Jesus' blood has made you free from the law of sin and death. Jesus has made us free from the curse of the law, but he has not redeemed us from the blessing of the law. What do I mean? Many see the Old Testament as the law, but they forget that many of our favorite scriptures are in the Old Testament, like Psalm 23. Although you're not under the law, the Old Testament is still very relevant to your life – not because it includes God's laws, but because it includes God's promises to you.

<u>Say it, Believe it, Think it, and Be It!</u>
I am free from the law of sin and death by Jesus Christ.

<u>Write Today's Promise</u>

_____

<u>Write Today's Confession</u>

_____

<u>What Do You Think about Today's Promise?</u>

_____

_____

Janice Hylton-Thompson

I Am Hidden in Christ

Colossians 3:3

For you died, and your life is hidden with Christ in God.

Christ died for everyone in the whole world. He paid the price for all of our sins, sicknesses, and diseases. When you accepted Christ, you experienced His death and resurrection with Him. Your old self died with Christ, and your new life is hidden in Him. When Christ rose from the dead, you rose up with Him and received the promise of eternal life in God's kingdom.

Since your life is hidden in Christ, focus on those things that honor the Lord. When God the Father looks at you, He does not see your sins, mistakes, and the wrong things that you do, but He sees His precious Son Jesus and His shed blood covering you. Walk in this truth that you are hidden in Christ.

<u>Say it, Believe it, Think it, and Be It!</u>
My life is hidden in Christ!

<u>Write Today's Promise</u>

_____

_____

<u>Write Today's Confession</u>

_____

_____

<u>What Do You Think about Today's Promise?</u>

_____

_____

In Christ I Am...

I Am Justified By Faith

Romans 5:1

Therefore, having been justified by faith, we have peace with God through our Lord Jesus Christ.

To be justified means 'just as if you have never sinned.' Now that you are born again, you are alive in Christ. Therefore, when God sees you, He sees you 'just as if you have never sinned' because He sees you through the blood of Christ. You have been justified by your faith in Christ. As a result, you have peace with God, and this peace is through Jesus Christ. Since God sees you as being justified now, it is important for you to think this way too. Do not think about your sins or the bad and wrong things you have done. God has made you justified in every area of your life. He has made you free from your past. Walk, think, believe, and talk like Christ because He has justified you.

<u>Say it, Believe it, Think it, and Be It!</u>
I am justified by faith, and I have peace with God through Jesus Christ.

<u>Write Today's Promise</u>

_____

_____

<u>Write Today's Confession</u>

_____

_____

<u>What Do You Think about Today's Promise?</u>

_____

_____

Janice Hylton-Thompson

I Am a Purchased Prize

Ephesians 1:13-14

In Him you also trusted, after you heard the word of truth, the gospel of your salvation; in whom also, having believed, you were sealed with the Holy Spirit of promise, who is the guarantee of our inheritance until the redemption of the purchased possession, to the praise of His glory.

Did you know that God purchased you with the precious blood of Jesus Christ? Yes! And, because of this, you are known as his purchased possession. You should get highly excited whenever you read this verse, because God loves you so much that He sacrificed His beloved Son, Jesus Christ, to buy you back from sin. So, in those times when you feel worthless, or you are not happy with yourself, or someone at school says something mean to you, remember that you are a purchased possession. If you are being picked on by a bully, remember that God paid a price for you and that you are important. Think on some of these verses that God placed in the Bible to remind you of who you are.

Say it, Believe it, Think it, and Be It!

I am a purchased possession, and I am important to God.

Write Today's Promise

_____

_____

Write Today's Confession

_____

_____

What Do You Think about Today's Promise?

_____

_____

In Christ I Am...

I Belong to God

1 Corinthians 6:20

For you were bought at a price; therefore glorify God in your body and in your spirit, which are God's.

Have you ever purchased or received an extremely expensive gift? Well, Christ purchased you back from the enemy, and the price He paid was His life when He shed His precious blood. The term we use for this is 'redeemed.' 'Redeemed' means to buy back. That is what God did for you: he bought you back from the devil. Remember, only those who have accepted Jesus can be called children of God, which means everyone else is a child of the devil. But God in His mercy sent Jesus, His son, to die for our sins and redeem us or buy us back from the devil. Because Christ bought you with His life, His desire is that you live for Him with your whole life, body, soul, and spirit.

<u>Say it, Believe it, Think it, and Be It!</u>

I was bought with a price so I will live for God with my body, soul, and spirit because I belong to God.

<u>Write Today's Promise</u>

_____

_____

<u>Write Today's Confession</u>

_____

_____

<u>What Do You Think about Today's Promise?</u>

_____

_____

Janice Hylton-Thompson

I Am Sealed With the Holy Spirit

Ephesians 1:13

In Him you also trusted, after you heard the word of truth, the gospel of your salvation; in whom also, having believed, you were sealed with the Holy Spirit of promise.

The Holy Spirit is the third person of the Trinity. There is God the Father, Jesus the Son, and the Holy Spirit, who is our comforter, teacher, and keeper. In this verse, Paul explains that, because you heard the good news of Jesus and responded with faith in Him, you are sealed with the Holy Spirit. This means the Holy Spirit has approved of you and has put his seal of promise on you — a promise of eternal life with the Lord. You don't have to worry about being good enough for God, or about Him rejecting you because you've messed up too much. He gave you his promise through the Holy Spirit, and He will make sure you get the eternal life that Jesus purchased for you.

Say it, Believe it, Think it, and Be It!

I am sealed with the Holy Spirit of promise because of the blood of Jesus Christ.

Write Today's Promise

_____
_____

Write Today's Confession

_____
_____

What Do You Think about Today's Promise?

_____
_____

In Christ I Am...
I Am Holy and Without Blame

Ephesians 1:4

Just as He chose us in Him before the foundation of the world, that we should be holy and without blame before Him in love.

God chose you and saved you, and you are now His child, which makes you 'holy.' We do not often use the word 'holy' to describe ourselves. We usually describe only God as 'holy.' However, according to this verse, God has chosen you to be holy. 'Holy' means to be set apart for God's use and purpose. It also means to be like God — to think like Him and to agree with His word. Say what God says and think like Him. Being 'holy' is to be Christ-minded. He chose you to be holy and without blame before Him so beginning today, walk in your holiness.

<u>Say it, Believe it, Think it, and Be It!</u>
I am holy!

<u>Write Today's Promise</u>

_____

_____

<u>Write Today's Confession</u>

_____

_____

<u>What Do You Think about Today's Promise?</u>

_____

_____

Janice Hylton-Thompson

I Am Healed

Isaiah 53:5

But He was wounded for our transgressions, He was bruised for our iniquities; the chastisement for our peace was upon Him, and by His stripes we are healed.

There might be times when your body will come under attack from sickness. It could be a headache, a sports injury, the flu, or cold. But always remember that Jesus died for you so that you can be healed. Sickness is an attack from the enemy, but Jesus took care of it before the world was formed. Even though Jesus took care of our sins, it is important for us to remember that we live in a fallen world where there is sickness and diseases, trials and tribulations.

Revelation 13:8 states, "And all that dwell upon the earth shall worship him, whose names are not written in the Book of Life of the Lamb, slain from the foundation of the world." In effect, this verse says that before Adam sinned, God already took care of his and our sin. When Christ was being beaten before his crucifixion, he was struck thirty-nine times. Every time those soldiers hit Him, He took on your sickness and diseases. Walk in your healing, say that you are healed, and believe it.

<u>Say it, Believe it, Think it, and Be It!</u>
I am healed by the stripes of Jesus Christ.

<u>Write Today's Promise</u>

_____

_____

<u>Write Today's Confession</u>

_____

_____

<u>What Do You Think about Today's Promise?</u>

_____

_____

In Christ I Am...

I Am Whole

Mark 5:34

And he said unto her, Daughter, thy faith hath made thee whole; go in peace, and be whole of thy plague. {KJV}

There is a victorious story about a woman with an issue of blood recorded in Mark 5. She had a bleeding problem for twelve long years. She went to all the doctors she could find, and spent all of her money, but no one was able to help her. She was still sick and now she had no money - she was broke! One day she heard that Jesus was passing by, and she thought to herself that if she could only touch the bottom of his robe, she would be healed. When Jesus came by, she fought her way through the crowd to touch Him, and she was healed. Jesus knew that someone had touched him, and he turned around and saw her. Then he told her that her faith had made her whole, and that she could go in peace and be whole of her plague. Notice that Jesus said she was whole.

Sometimes, things happen in your lives that affect your entire being. They might affect you mentally, emotionally, or physically. But when Jesus heals, He desires to heal all of those parts of you. So if there is something going on in your life and you believe that God can heal and deliver you, then you also need to confess that you are whole in the name of Jesus!

<u>Say it, Believe it, Think it, and Be It</u>

I am whole!

<u>Write Today's Promise</u>

_____

_____

<u>Write Today's Confession</u>

_____

_____

<u>What Do You Think about Today's Promise?</u>

_____

_____

Note!

Since the Bible tells one story from start to finish, the story of our fall and our redemption through Christ, the blessings you've learned in this section can be used interchangeably in any of the five categories. You can mix-and-match however you like. There's no right or wrong way to speak God's Word over your life!

Salvation Confession

I am crucified with Christ, because I am redeemed through Christ's blood, and I am forgiven. I am saved by grace. I am delivered because I am born of God, and I am a gift from God, therefore I am alive to God.

I am known by God because I am His child. I am free from the law because I am hidden in Christ. I am justified by faith and I am a purchased prize. Therefore, I belong to God, I am sealed with the Holy Spirit, I am holy without blame, I am healed and I am whole!

Janice Hylton-Thompson

THE NEW ME

John 3:1-17

¹There was a man of the Pharisees named Nicodemus, a ruler of the Jews.

²This man came to Jesus by night and said to Him, "Rabbi, we know that You are a teacher come from God; for no one can do these signs that You do unless God is with him."

³Jesus answered and said to him, "Most assuredly, I say to you, unless one is born again, he cannot see the kingdom of God."

⁴Nicodemus said to Him, "How can a man be born when he is old? Can he enter a second time into his mother's womb and be born?"

⁵Jesus answered, "Most assuredly, I say to you, unless one is born of water and the Spirit, he cannot enter the kingdom of God. ⁶That which is born of the flesh is flesh, and that which is born of the Spirit is spirit. ⁷Do not marvel that I said to you, 'You must be born again.' ⁸The wind blows where it wishes, and you hear the sound of it, but cannot tell where it comes from and where it goes. So is everyone who is born of the Spirit."

⁹Nicodemus answered and said to Him, "How can these things be?"

¹⁰Jesus answered and said to him, "Are you the teacher of Israel, and do not know these things? ¹¹Most assuredly, I say to you, We speak what We know and testify what We have seen, and you do not receive Our witness.

¹²If I have told you earthly things and you do not believe, how will you believe if I tell you heavenly things? ¹³No one has ascended to heaven but He who came down from heaven, that is, the Son of Man who is in heaven. ¹⁴And as Moses lifted up the serpent in the wilderness, even so must the Son of Man be lifted up, ¹⁵that whoever believes in Him should not perish but have eternal life. ¹⁶For God so loved the world that He gave His only begotten Son, that whoever believes in Him should not perish but have everlasting life. ¹⁷For God did not send His Son into the world to condemn the world, but that the world through Him might be saved.

In Christ I Am...

I Am Redeemed From the Curse of the Law

Galatians 3:13

Christ has redeemed us from the curse of the law, having become a curse for us (for it is written, "Cursed is everyone who hangs on a tree.")

Redeemed means to 'buy back,' and it is a price that is paid for someone's freedom. At one time, we were all slaves to sin because of our choice to rebel against what we knew was right and do whatever we wanted instead. God loved us so much that he sacrificed His only begotten Son, Jesus Christ, for all people. When Christ died, he became a curse for us so that we would be cursed no more. Christ paid the ultimate price for our freedom - his life and sinless blood. Christ has redeemed us or bought us back from the curse of the law of sin and death. That makes you an extremely expensive gift! So you have been redeemed, you are a purchased possession, and you are worthy to God. You mean something very special to God.

<u>Say it, Believe it, Think it, and Be It!</u>

I am redeemed from the curse of the law of sin and death.

<u>Write Today's Promise</u>

_____

_____

<u>Write Today's Confession</u>

_____

_____

<u>What Do You Think about Today's Promise?</u>

_____

_____

Janice Hylton-Thompson

I Am the Seed of Abraham

Galatians 3:29

And if you are Christ's, then you are Abraham's seed, and heirs according to the promise.

Abraham is known as the father of the Jewish people. God chose Abraham, blessed him, and promised him that all of his seed would be blessed. In the Biblical days, unless you were a Jew, you were not considered to be of the seed of Abraham. However, Jesus Christ came from the seed of Abraham, and when you made Jesus Christ the Lord of your life, you instantly became a seed, or a descendant, of Abraham as well.

Therefore, all of the promises that God gave Abraham now belongs to you. Abraham was a great, mighty, and wealthy man. God blessed Abraham because God chose to bless him. Now, because of Jesus Christ, you can enjoy the blessings of Abraham. The blessings of Abraham can be found in Genesis 12:1-3. [1] Now the Lord had said to Abram: "Get out of your country, From your family And from your father's house,To a land that I will show you. [2] I will make you a great nation;I will bless you And make your name great; And you shall be a blessing. [3] I will bless those who bless you, And I will curse him who curses you; And in you all the families of the earth shall be blessed."

<u>Say it, Believe it, Think it, and Be It!</u>
I am Abraham's seed or descendant.

<u>Write Today's Promise</u>

___

___

<u>Write Today's Confession</u>

___

___

<u>What Do You Think about Today's Promise?</u>

___

___

In Christ I Am...

I Am a Chosen Generation

1 Peter 2:9

But you are a chosen generation, a royal priesthood, a holy nation, His own special people, that you may proclaim the praises of Him who called you out of darkness into His marvelous light.

In the Old Testament, there were high priests who went to God on behalf of the people for their sins. Ordinary people like you and me were not allowed to approach God directly; we had to go through a priest. However, when Christ came, He took the place of the high priests, and became the sacrifice that the priests would make. God has chosen you because of Christ's death. You are now a chosen generation and a royal priesthood that was handpicked by God. You are now a holy nation, chosen, and set aside by God. You can have your own relationship with God, and you can talk to Him and hear from Him directly. You are God's special young man or woman.

Say it, Believe it, Think it, and Be It!

I am chosen by the Lord. I am a chosen generation, a royal priesthood, a holy nation, I am special to the Lord.

Write Today's Promise

_____

_____

Write Today's Confession

_____

_____

What Do You Think about Today's Promise?

_____

_____

Janice Hylton-Thompson

I Am A New Creation

1 Corinthians 5:17

Therefore, if anyone is in Christ, he is a new creation; old things have passed away; behold, all things have become new.

When you came to Christ, you became a brand-new creation, or a new person. That is what it means to be born again — to become new in Christ. All of the old things that you were have been erased. The blood of Jesus has washed them away and all things have become new. This means that in Christ, you have a new personality. The old you is gone, and Jesus is building a brand-new person out of you. You were a sinner because of Adam, but now you are a saint because of Jesus. Isn't that exciting?

<u>Say it, Believe it, Think it, and Be It!</u>
I am a new person in Jesus Christ.

<u>Write Today's Promise</u>

_____

_____

<u>Write Today's Confession</u>

_____

_____

<u>What Do You Think about Today's Promise?</u>

_____

_____

In Christ I Am...

I Am in God's Family

1 Corinthians 12:27

Now you are the body of Christ, and members individually.

The Body of Christ is made up of all of us who became born again by asking Jesus to come into our hearts and live with us. This makes up the Body of Christ, or the family of God. Since you have asked Jesus to come into your heart, you are now a member of God's family. The Body of Christ is your brothers and sisters in the Lord. That means it's important to be a part of a local church, because the people in your church can help you or can give you advice whenever you need it. Even though you are a member of the Body of Christ, God knows you as a person. He cares about everything that concerns you and He loves you.

<u>Say it, Believe it, Think it, and Be It!</u>

I am a part of the body of Christ, and I am a part of God's family.

<u>Write Today's Promise</u>

_____

_____

<u>Write Today's Confession</u>

_____

_____

<u>What Do You Think about Today's Promise?</u>

_____

_____

Janice Hylton-Thompson

I Am a Child of God

Galatians 3:26

For you are all sons of God through faith in Christ Jesus.

This verse is similar to John 3:12, which states "But as many as received Him, to them He gave the right to become children of God, to those who believe in His name." Children of God and sons of God mean the same thing. Here, the Apostle Paul is telling you that you are a 'son' or a 'child' of God because you have put your faith in Jesus Christ. 'Sonship' gives you power and authority to speak the Word of the Lord.

Begin to think of God as your Heavenly Father. When you pray, begin your prayer with "Father..." Your Heavenly Father loves you so much and wants to have a relationship and a friendship with you. Take time to pray and get to know Him. He wants you to come to Him with your questions, desires, hopes, fears, dreams, and anything else on your mind. Why do you not spend some time alone with God, your Heavenly Father, today? He always wants to spend time with you, and He waits patiently for you to come and spend time with Him.

<u>Say it, Believe it, Think it, and Be It!</u>

I am a child of God.

<u>Write Today's Promise</u>

_____

_____

<u>Write Today's Confession</u>

_____

_____

<u>What Do You Think about Today's Promise?</u>

_____

_____

In Christ I Am...

I Am a Friend of God
Part 1

John 15:14

You are my friends if you do whatever I command you.

It is so awesome to know that Jesus has made you His friend. In this verse, Jesus says that you are His friend if you do what He tells you to do in the Bible. You will only know what God has said in His Word by reading it and attending church regularly. In verse 15, Jesus goes on to say that he no longer calls his disciples and you servants, but He calls them friends. You are Jesus' friend; you are a friend of God.

Say it, Believe it, Think it, and Be It!

Jesus is my best friend and I am Jesus' best friend. He shares the secret of His Word, the Bible, with me.

Write Today's Promise

_____
_____

Write Today's Confession

_____
_____

What Do You Think about Today's Promise?

_____
_____

Janice Hylton-Thompson

I Am a Friend of God
Part 2

John 15:15

No longer do I call you servants, for a servant does not know what his master is doing; but I have called you friends, for all things that I heard from My Father I have made known to you.

There is a song called "I Am a Friend of God." It is a beautiful song that reminds us that we are now friends of God and not strangers. When you have a friend, you will talk to and share things with that friend. Some things you can only share with that special friend, because you know that your friend has your back. Well, this friend is Jesus! Make Jesus your best friend. Talk to Him every day and share everything with Him. Jesus is the only friend that will be with you always. So, love Him and spend time alone with Him.

<u>Say it, Believe it, Think it, and Be It!</u>
I am a friend of God.

<u>Write Today's Promise</u>

_____

_____

<u>Write Today's Confession</u>

_____

_____

<u>What Do You Think about Today's Promise?</u>

_____

_____

In Christ I Am...

I Am the Righteousness of Christ
Part 1

2 Corinthians 5:21

For He made Him who knew no sin to be sin for us,
that we might become the righteousness of God in Him.

    Corinthians was written by the Apostle Paul, who also wrote most of the New Testament. Before he came to know Jesus, he used to kill Christians because they believed in Jesus Christ. One day, while Paul was on his way to Damascus to kill more Christians, he met the resurrected Jesus and fell. Paul invited Jesus into his heart, and he became a changed man. Paul invited Jesus into his heart because Paul realized that he was a sinner and needed a savior, which was Jesus Christ. This tells us that though we all have a past, it does not matter. If we invite Jesus into our hearts, He will change us and forgive us of our sins.

<u>Say it, Believe it, Think it, and Be It!</u>
I am the righteousness of Christ.

<u>Write Today's Promise</u>

_____
_____

<u>Write Today's Confession</u>

_____
_____

<u>What Do You Think about Today's Promise?</u>

_____
_____

Janice Hylton-Thompson

I Am the Righteousness of Christ Part 2

2 Corinthians 5:21

For He made Him who knew no sin to be sin for us, that we might become the righteousness of God in Him.

The Apostle Paul, the author of 2 Corinthians, really understood what it meant to become the righteousness of Christ. Think about how much guilt Paul must have had because of all the Christians he killed before he met Jesus! When Paul asked Jesus to come into his heart, though, he understood that he was no longer the man who used to kill Christians. He understood and knew that he was now the righteousness of Christ. In other words, Paul was now in right standing with God. Christ took Paul's place on the cross so that he could become like Christ. Christ also took your place on the cross so that you could become like Him. When Christ died and became sin, he took all sin, sickness, and disease upon and within Him. Therefore, you are able to become righteous like Christ. Thus, you are the righteousness of Christ because in His death, He has made you to be in right standing with God.

<u>Say it, Believe it, Think it, and Be It!</u>
I am the righteousness of Christ.

<u>Write Today's Promise</u>

_____

_____

<u>Write Today's Confession</u>

_____

_____

<u>What Do You Think about Today's Promise?</u>

_____

_____

In Christ I Am...

I Am Righteous

Psalm 5:12

*For You, O Lord, will bless the righteous;
with favor you will surround him as with a shield.*

Earlier we talked about how you are the righteousness of Christ! Because you are now the righteousness of God, you can call yourself righteous. To be righteous means to be in right standing with God. You are in right standing with God because Jesus died for you, and you made him the Lord of your life. You are not righteous because of anything you have done, but it is because of what Christ has done for you. God has surrounded you with a shield because you are righteous. This shield is large enough to cover your whole body from every direction. God has surrounded you with His love, protection, grace, mercy, and favor. Additionally, He has covered your soul, which consists of your will, intellect and emotions. So not only has God made you righteous, but He has also surrounded you with His shield.

<u>Say it, Believe it, Think it, and Be It!</u>

I am righteous, and God has blessed me with favor that covers me like a shield.

<u>Write Today's Promise</u>

_____

_____

<u>Write Today's Confession</u>

_____

_____

<u>What Do You Think about Today's Promise?</u>

_____

_____

Janice Hylton-Thompson
I Am a Witness for Christ

Acts 1:8

But you shall receive power when the Holy Spirit has come upon you; and you shall be witnesses to me in Jerusalem, and in all Judea and Samaria, and to the end of the earth."

Before Jesus went up to heaven, He encouraged His followers to remain in Jerusalem until they received the Promise of the Father, which is the Holy Spirit. With the indwelling of the Holy Spirit, Jesus' disciples would be able to be witnesses to the world. The same goes for you today. The Holy Spirit is a gift that is available to you. The Bible lists many amazing things that the Holy Spirit's power can do inside you. You can get spiritual gifts, which are almost like superpowers. You can find supernatural courage and strength when you feel overwhelmed. You have access to peace and comfort even when life gets crazy. All of this power is inside you already; you just have to ask God to activate it. If you are not filled with the Holy Spirit, you can receive Him today by asking. With the Holy Spirit living on the inside, you will be able to be a witness or an example for Jesus Christ.

<u>Say it, Believe it, Think it, and Be It!</u>
I am a witness for the Lord Jesus Christ.

<u>Write Today's Promise</u>

_____

_____

<u>Write Today's Confession</u>

_____

_____

<u>What Do You Think about Today's Promise?</u>

_____

_____

In Christ I Am...

I Am Blameless

Ephesians 1:4

Just as He chose us in Him before the foundation of the world, that we should be holy and without blame before Him in love.

What comes to mind when you hear the word 'blame' or 'blameless'? If you're blameless for a certain action, it means you don't have any fault or guilt for what happened. When you stand before God, He will not put blame on you for your sins or mistakes. Why? Because when Jesus was on the cross, God the Father placed all of your sins upon and within Him. Because of this, you are blameless in the eyes of God. Even though God has made you blameless, the enemy will make you think that you are not. The enemy will put things in your mind; to make you think that you are not who God has called you to be. Regardless of this, remember, you are who God says you are. That is why it is important for you to know who you are in Christ. This book is a great tool to help you learn your new identity.

<u>Say it, Believe it, Think it, and Be It!</u>
I am blameless in the sight of the Lord!

<u>Write Today's Promise</u>

_____

_____

<u>Write Today's Confession</u>

_____

_____

<u>What Do You Think about Today's Promise?</u>

_____

_____

Janice Hylton-Thompson

I Am Just

Proverbs 4:18

But the path of the just is like the shining sun, that shines ever brighter unto the perfect day.

'Just' is a word that is similar to the word justified, which means 'just as if you have never sinned.' Through Christ you have become just or justified. Your path is like the shining sun. Have you ever taken some time to watch the rising of the sun? It begins with a little light, but as time passes, it grows bigger and brighter. As you walk with Jesus, that is how your path will be. Every day, it will be brighter and brighter because Jesus is that light that continues to shine. Continue to walk in Christ every day, and he will lead you in the right path. Walk in the Word and the truth of God's Word.

<u>Say it, Believe it, Think it, and Be It!</u>
I am 'just' and walk in the path of the Lord

<u>Write Today's Promise</u>

_____

_____

<u>Write Today's Confession</u>

_____

_____

<u>What Do You Think about Today's Promise?</u>

_____

_____

In Christ I Am...

I Am God's Workmanship

Ephesians 2:10

For we are His workmanship, created in Christ Jesus for good works, which God prepared beforehand that we should walk in them.

It is important to know that none of us are perfect; we all continue to sin and make mistakes, because we're still growing. Nevertheless, we are God's workshop, meaning that He is working in us daily. What are some of the good works we can do? One important starting point is to attend church regularly. There you can participate in various church activities such as singing in the youth choir, dancing in the praise dance ministry for the glory and honor of God, feeding the hungry, clothing the naked. It is important to remember that none of these things saves us because salvation comes only through the blood of Jesus Christ and his grace, but we should still do things to bless others because of all the ways God is blessing us.

You see, God has already prepared you to do good works. He has a calling upon your life, and He wants you to desire His will and destiny for your life. Therefore, I encourage you to walk in God's will for your life. Do not allow the plans of the enemy to take over your life.

<u>Say it, Believe it, Think it, and Be It!</u>

I am God's workmanship, and God is working in me every day.

<u>Write Today's Promise</u>

_____

_____

<u>Write Today's Confession</u>

_____

_____

<u>What Do You Think about Today's Promise?</u>

_____

_____

Janice Hylton-Thompson

I Am the House of God

1 Corinthians 3:16

Do you not know that you are the temple of God and that the Spirit of God dwells in you?

Did you know that when you asked Jesus to come into your heart, you became born again, or saved? Since Jesus is living inside you, you are now the house of God. Think about your church. There are some things that would not be appropriate to do in your church. Well, it is the same thing with your body or the House of God. Take care of your body by doing things such as eating healthy, drinking lots of water, exercising, and taking a bath or shower. Make every effort to not do things that can be unhealthy for your body including smoking, drinking, having pre-marital sex, taking drugs, and the like. Taking care of your body helps God bless you in more ways. There are things you can do with a healthy body, such as going on a missions trip, helping to build a house, or going on vacations to exotic places, which you couldn't do with an unhealthy body. The healthier you are, the more ways there are for you to enjoy God's creation!

Say it, Believe it, Think it, and Be It!
I am the house of the Lord, and He is living in me.

Write Today's Promise

_____

_____

Write Today's Confession

_____

_____

What Do You Think about Today's Promise?

_____

_____

In Christ I Am...

I Am Complete in Christ

Colossians 2:9-10

For in Him dwells all the fullness of the Godhead bodily; and you are complete in Him, who is the head of all principality and power.

The Godhead, or Trinity, is made up of God the Father, God the Son, which is Jesus, and God the Holy Spirit. They are not three gods, but one God that has three different functions. God the Father is the loving father that gave His Son Jesus for us all. Jesus is the manifestation or the form of the Godhead that came to die for us. The Holy Spirit is our comforter and teacher, who will teach us all things. In the same way the fullness of the Godhead is in Jesus Christ, so the fullness of Christ dwells in you once He becomes the Lord of your life.

Others will sometimes try to make you think that there is something missing in you, that you need the latest fashions to be complete, or that you're losing out if you're not watching the same movies and listening to the same music as your friends. However, in Christ, you are complete—nothing broken and nothing missing. Your salvation is complete in Christ. Your healing, peace, favor, and protection are complete in Christ. God has completely met all of your needs in Christ. In other words, everything you need, God has already provided through Christ.

<u>Say it, Believe it, Think it, and Be It</u>

I am complete in Christ, nothing broken and nothing missing.

<u>Write Today's Promise</u>

_____

_____

<u>Write Today's Confession</u>

_____

_____

<u>What Do You Think about Today's Promise?</u>

_____

_____

Janice Hylton-Thompson

I Am a Joint Heir with Christ

Romans 8:17

...and if children, then heirs—heirs of God and joint heirs with Christ, if indeed we suffer with Him, that we may also be glorified together.

A good way to understand the term 'heir' is to think of the princes of England — William, Harry, and now, George. In the same way that they are heirs to the throne, you are a joint heir with Christ too. The princes have to wait to become kings, but you are kings right now because you are in Jesus. This means that you are seated with Him now, and you are ruling and reigning with Him right now. Isn't that amazing?

Say it, Believe it, Think it, and Be It!
I am joint heir with Christ. I am ruling and reigning with Him.

Write Today's Promise

_____

_____

Write Today's Confession

_____

_____

What Do You Think about Today's Promise?

_____

_____

In Christ I Am...

I Am Seated with Christ

Ephesians 2:6

**And raised us up together, and made us sit together
in the heavenly places in Christ Jesus.**

Before we came to Jesus Christ, we were all condemned to hell. However, because we came to Christ for salvation, Jesus raised us up from hell and we are now seated together with Him. Not only did He raise us up from the depths of hell, but He also made us sit together with Him in the heavenly places. Therefore, do not allow anyone to bring you down from where Christ has you seated with Him. Do not allow anyone to make you sad, brokenhearted, or depressed. Even in your most trying times, hold your head up, and look to your Heavenly Father who has raised you up. You are seated on the right hand of God the Father in Jesus. The phrase 'right hand of God' speaks of power and authority. Christ has given you His power and authority to speak those things that you want to see happen in your life. Go right ahead and use your power and authority!

Say it, Believe it, Think it, and Be It!

I am raised up with Jesus and seated with Christ in heavenly places.

Write Today's Promise

_____
_____

Write Today's Confession

_____
_____

What Do You Think about Today's Promise?

_____
_____

Janice Hylton-Thompson

I Am a Faithful Saint

Ephesians 1:1

Paul, an apostle of Jesus Christ by the will of God, to the saints who are in Ephesus, and faithful in Christ Jesus:

The book of Ephesians is my favorite book in the Bible. It tells a lot about who we have become in Christ since we have made Him the Lord of our lives. In this world, people are considered either sinners or saints. Here, the Apostle Paul addressed the body of Christ as saints. Since you are saved, or born again, you are a saint. Not only did he address you as a saint, but he also called you faithful. Faithful simply means that you walk by faith in Jesus Christ. You were able to be born again because you had faith in the work that Jesus Christ completed on the Cross. So remember that not only are you a saint and a believer in Jesus Christ, but you also walk and believe by faith in Jesus Christ.

Say it, Believe it, Think it, and Be It!
I am a Saint, and I am faithful.

Write Today's Promise

_____

_____

Write Today's Confession

_____

_____

What Do You Think about Today's Promise?

_____

_____

In Christ I Am...

I Am an Ambassador for Christ

2 Corinthians 5:20

Now then, we are ambassadors for Christ, as though God were pleading through us: we implore you on Christ's behalf, be reconciled to God.

Let us focus on the first portion of this verse: "Now then, we are ambassadors for Christ..." An ambassador is someone who represents another person, or someone who goes somewhere on behalf of another. Think of the President of the United States of America, who has ambassadors or representatives who go to other countries and speak on the President's behalf. The important thing to remember is that the ambassador is to only say what the President says. In the same way, you are encouraged to only say what Jesus said. How will you know what Jesus said? By reading, studying and meditating on His Word, the Bible. You can also read books like this one, which explain what the Bible says. In this book, you are learning who you are in Christ. So when someone calls you names or says mean things about you, knowing who you are in Christ will help you to recognize those mean things as lies from the enemy. For example, if someone calls you ugly, you will remember that God has made you beautiful. But if you do not know that God said in his word that you are beautiful, the mean things they say about you will stay in your heart. Remember to speak God's Word over every situation.

<u>Say it, Believe it, Think it, and Be It!</u>
I am an ambassador for Christ! I represent Christ!

<u>Write Today's Promise</u>

_____

_____

<u>Write Today's Confession</u>

_____

_____

<u>What Do You Think about Today's Promise?</u>

_____

_____

Janice Hylton-Thompson

I Am the Head and Not the Tail
Above Only and Not Beneath

Deuteronomy 28:13

And the Lord will make you the head and not the tail; you shall be above only, and not be beneath, if you heed the commandments of the Lord your God, which I command you today, and are careful to observe them.

God chose Israel as His special people. He wanted them to be separated and set aside for His purpose and will. God wanted Israel to be the head and not the tail. God wants the same for you today. God's desire is that you will recognize and walk in the favor that He has blessed you with. You are the head and not the tail; you shall be above always and never beneath. Whenever you try something new, believe that God will grant you success. If you step out on faith and do something God says to do, even though it's scary and people might make fun of you, remind yourself that He has already spoken His approval over you. You don't need to fear what other people will say or think, because God's opinion is the only one that matters. Everywhere you go and in all that you do, remember who God has called you to be.

Say it, Believe it, Think it, and Be It!
I am the head and not the tail; I shall be above only and not beneath.

Write Today's Promise

_____

_____

Write Today's Confession

_____

_____

What Do You Think about Today's Promise?

_____

_____

In Christ I Am...
Faith Is Always Now

Hebrews 11:1

Now faith is the substance of things hoped for, the evidence of things not seen.

I wanted to take a break from our normal way of studying and take a look at a very familiar verse that is used to describe faith. We will take a look at a few words that are mentioned. The first word is 'now.' What does 'now' mean to you? The second word is 'substance.' 'Substance' is something that is physical. Next is the phrase 'things hoped for,' which means something that doesn't exist yet, something that only exists in your hopes and dreams. The next word is 'evidence', which means proof. The last phrase is 'not seen', which means you cannot see it, or that it is invisible to you.

When we put it all together, we see that FAITH is now, and it is the physical thing that you are hoping for. Your faith is the proof that you have what you do not see with your physical eyes. Faith is always now, not yesterday or tomorrow, but right now. Whatever you believe in God for, God has already given it to you, and all you have to do is to receive it in Jesus' name.

If you believe in God to heal your body, do not say, "God is going to heal me." 'Going to' is in the future and is not faith.

Instead, say I am healed in Jesus' name. You see, faith is now! Faith speaks what God speaks, thinks what God thinks, and believes what God believes. God thinks, believes, and says that you are healed now, today, at this very moment, because faith is NOW!

<u>Say it, Believe it, Think it, and Be It!</u>
I will speak what God speaks over me, because faith is now!

<u>Write Today's Promise</u>

<u>Write Today's Confession</u>

<u>What Do You Think about Today's Promise?</u>

The New Me Confession

I am redeemed from the curse of the Law because I am the seed of Abraham. I am a chosen generation, a new creation, I am in God's family and I am His child!

I am a friend of God, the righteousness of Christ, and I am righteous! Therefore, I am a witness for Christ.

I am blameless, I am just, I am God's workmanship, and I am the house of God. I am complete in Christ, joint heirs with Him, and I am seated with Him.

I am a faithful servant, an ambassador for Christ. Therefore, I am the head and not the tail, I shall be above only and not beneath, because faith is always now!!

Janice Hylton-Thompson
GOD LOVES ME

One of the first bible verses I remember learning as a little girl, taught in Sunday school by my Sunday school teacher Ms. B was **1 John 4:7-8**. She taught it to us in a song and I never forgot these two verses. I love this portion of scripture, because it talks about God's love for us and His Word to love others.

1 John 4:7-11

⁷Beloved, let us love one another, for love is of God; and everyone who loves is born of God and knows God. ⁸He who does not love does not know God, for God is love. ⁹In this the love of God was manifested toward us, that God has sent His only begotten Son into the world, that we might live through Him. ¹⁰In this is love, not that we loved God, but that He loved us and sent His Son to be the propitiation for our sins. ¹¹Beloved, if God so loved us, we also ought to love one another.

John 3:16

For God so loved the world that he gave his only begotten son, that whoever believes in him should not perish but have everlasting life.

In Christ I Am...

I Am Created for God

Revelation 4:11

You are worthy, O Lord, to receive glory and honor and power; for you created all things, and by your will they exist and were created.

The Apostle John, also known as the disciple whom Jesus loved, acknowledges here that God is worthy to receive glory, honor, and power. Why? God created all things, including you, for His will. When God created you, He had a purpose for you. God's first purpose is for you to invite Jesus Christ into your heart so that you can spend eternity with him.

Then His will is for you to share His love with others, and for you to live the rest of your life for Him, fulfilling His plans for you. Do you know what your destiny is while you are here on Earth? Do you know what you are supposed to be doing for the Kingdom of God? If you do not know what your purpose is on earth, pray and seek the Lord. He may not show you today or tomorrow, but if you keep praying and believing that He has an answer, you will be ready to receive His answer whenever He gives it.

Say it, Believe it, Think it, and Be It!
I am created for God.

Write Today's Promise

_____

_____

Write Today's Confession

_____

_____

What Do You Think about Today's Promise?

_____

_____

Janice Hylton-Thompson

I Am Chosen by God

John 15:16

You did not choose me, but I chose you and appointed you that you should go and bear fruit, and that your fruit should remain, that whatever you ask the Father in My name He may give you.

Let us focus only on the first part of this verse. Jesus said that He chose you and appointed you, or sent you to bear fruit or to be like Him. Think about it! Out of everyone in the world, God chose you to share His Word with others. You are so special and important to God that He chose you to bring His message of love to others who do not know Him. Remember that God does not choose you because you are better than other people, or because you did so many good deeds. Instead, God chose you because He loves you, and He sent His Son, Jesus, to die for your sins.

<u>Say it, Believe it, Think it, and Be It!</u>
I am chosen by God to share His love with others.

<u>Write Today's Promise</u>

_____

_____

<u>Write Today's Confession</u>

_____

_____

<u>What Do You Think about Today's Promise?</u>

_____

_____

In Christ I Am...

I Am Chosen In Christ

Ephesians 1:4

Just as He chose us in Him before the foundation of the world, that we should be holy and without blame before Him in love.

Have you ever been chosen for something like a team, or to perform a praise song or dance, or to do the favorite part in the Christmas show? How did that make you feel? Think of how God chose you before He created the heavens and the earth. Before God started making anything else, He chose you to be His child. That means you are very special and important to Him. Therefore, when you come before God the Father, you can come without blame. You can come to Him in faith without feeling guilty or condemned. There is no need to feel guilty of the things you have done, because Jesus already paid for all of the wrong and bad things you have done. God has chosen you to be holy and without blame before Him in Love.

<u>Say it, Believe it, Think it, and Be It!</u>
I am chosen by God!

<u>Write Today's Promise</u>

_____

_____

<u>Write Today's Confession</u>

_____

_____

<u>What Do You Think about Today's Promise?</u>

_____

_____

Janice Hylton-Thompson

I Am Wonderfully Made

Psalm 134:14

I will praise you, for I am fearfully and wonderfully made
Marvelous are your works, And that my soul knows very well.

This is a beautiful verse written by King David, whom God anointed as King when he was a teen. God wants you to know that you are fearfully and wonderfully made by Him; He carefully and lovingly crafted every part of you, putting you together just the way He wanted you, and He thinks you are great. David goes on to say that his soul knows that God created him. Like David, know and remember that God created you, and you are wonderful and great in the eyes of God.

<u>Say it, Believe it, Think it, and Be It!</u>
I am wonderfully made by God!

<u>Write Today's Promise</u>

_____

_____

<u>Write Today's Confession</u>

_____

_____

<u>What Do You Think about Today's Promise?</u>

_____

_____

In Christ I Am...
I Am the Apple of God's Eye
Psalm 17:8-9

Keep me as the apple of your eye; hide me under the shadow of your wings, from the wicked who oppress me, from my deadly enemies who surround me.

This is by far one of my favorite verses in the scriptures because it tells you how important you are to God. The apple of your eye is considered to be the most important and precious part of the eye — the pupil. David is asking the Lord to keep him as the most important part of His eye. The same applies to you today. You are so special and important to God that he keeps you as the most important part of His eye. As a mother hen hides her chicks under her wings, so the Lord hides you under his wings of protection. He hides you from the devil, who comes to oppress and afflict you. The devil is out to kill, steal, and destroy, and he has surrounded you with deadly weapons. If you think about the devil too much, it's easy to get very scared and to begin living in fear of him or the pain he can bring. But fear not; God is already surrounding you, and no weapon formed against you shall prosper. You are the apple of God's eye and He has His eyes on you. Wherever you go, whatever you do, God is keeping His eyes on you, to protect you from the plans of the enemy.

<u>Say it, Believe it, Think it, and Be It!</u>
I am the apple of God's eye; he hides me under his wings and surrounds me from the wicked and deadly enemies.

<u>Write Today's Promise</u>

_____

_____

<u>Write Today's Confession</u>

_____

_____

<u>What Do You Think about Today's Promise?</u>

_____

_____

Janice Hylton-Thompson
I Am Taught of the Lord
Isaiah 54:13

**All your children shall be taught by the Lord,
and great shall be the peace of your children.**

God promised parents that their children will be taught by the Lord and that they will have peace. You will be taught of the Lord, which means that He will help you understand what you read in the Bible, and He will show you moments in your everyday life that teach you more about how He works. As he does this, you'll find that you have peace. When you are taught the Word of God, whether by human teachers or by God Himself, you will see how blessed you are in every area of your life. This book is a perfect example of how you can be taught the Word of God about who you are in Christ.

You can also be taught by reading the different stories in the Bible and other Christian books. You can also go to Sunday school, youth church, etc. Being taught God's Word will bring you peace, joy, blessings, answers, and much more – you have to experience it to believe it!

<u>Say it, Believe it, Think it, and Be It!</u>
I am taught of the Lord, and I have great peace in every area of my life.

<u>Write Today's Promise</u>

_____

_____

<u>Write Today's Confession</u>

_____

_____

<u>What Do You Think about Today's Promise?</u>

_____

_____

In Christ I Am...
I Am Filled With the Fullness of God
Ephesians 3:19

**To know the love of Christ which passes knowledge;
that you may be filled with all the fullness of God.**

The love of Christ is something that cannot be comprehended, or even compared to any other experience. His love is unconditional, which means there is nothing you can do to make him him stop loving you. Also, there is nothing you can do to make God love you any more than he already does. His love will never change just because you have sinned or missed the mark. God is love, and He loves you regardless of your mistakes. The term 'to know' in this verse is the same word used when the Bible said in Genesis 4:1 that Adam 'knew' his wife. In other words, Adam and Eve became one. It is the same way, God wants us to become one with Him. He wants us to know Him intimately, to know Him so well that we never doubt His love or mercy, to know beyond a shadow of a doubt that His plans for us are the very best plans anyone could possibly make.

<u>Say it, Believe it, Think it, and Be It!</u>
I am saved by grace through faith in Jesus Christ.

<u>Write Today's Promise</u>

_____

_____

<u>Write Today's Confession</u>

_____

_____

<u>What Do You Think about Today's Promise?</u>

_____

_____

Janice Hylton-Thompson

I Am Accepted in The Beloved

Ephesians 1:6

*To the praise of the glory of His grace,
by which He made us accepted in the Beloved.*

Today's word is 'accepted!' Remember that God chose you before the foundation of the world to be holy and without blame. He also predestined and adopted you. In Christ, you are accepted by God.

This is very important because we are living in a time where, as teens, you are fighting against a lot of competing voices. Friends, celebrities, and total strangers will try to dictate everything about you, like what is a good weight, what kinds of clothes to wear, how to do your hair, what to watch and listen to, and everything you could imagine. Then, and only then, will you be accepted to their standards - until their standards suddenly change! However, God tells you that because you have made Jesus Christ the Lord of your life, you are accepted by Him. His is the only opinion that matters, because only His plan for your life will bring you ultimate satisfaction. God accepts you just the way you are. Look in the mirror and point to yourself, and tell yourself that God loves you for you. As long as you have made Jesus Christ the Lord of your life, you are perfect in God's eyes.

<u>Say it, Believe it, Think it, and Be It!</u>
I am accepted by God just the way I am!

<u>Write Today's Promise</u>

_____

_____

<u>Write Today's Confession</u>

_____

_____

<u>What Do You Think about Today's Promise?</u>

_____

_____

In Christ I Am...

I Am Loved by God

Ephesians 2:4-5

But God, who is rich in mercy, because of His great love with which He loved us, even when we were dead in trespasses, made us alive together with Christ (by grace you have been saved).

Today's verse talks about how, as a people, we were walking in sin, we spoke things that were not godly, and we were all children of disobedience. Before Christ, we did what we wanted to do, we thought how we wanted to think, and as a result were people who deserved God's judgment and punishment.

But God, who loved us so much, gave His Son Jesus for you and me and the whole world. God made us alive together in Christ, and it is by the grace of God that we are saved. No one can take the credit, and no one can say it is because of them that you are saved. Salvation comes by the grace and mercy of God. That mercy doesn't stop on the day you're saved; the same love that made Him pursue you even when you were a sinner guarantees that He will keep pursuing you until you trust Him and His plans for your life.

Say it, Believe it, Think it, and Be It!
I am loved by God I am made alive with Christ!

Write Today's Promise

_____

_____

Write Today's Confession

_____

_____

What Do You Think about Today's Promise?

_____

_____

Janice Hylton-Thompson

I Am Beloved

1 John 4:7

Beloved, let us love one another, for love is of God; and everyone who loves is born of God and knows God.

The Apostle John, also known as the disciple whom Jesus loves, wrote the letter we call 1 John. John used a lot of words that express God's love and emotions toward us. One of those words is 'beloved,' which means to be 'loved of God'. It is a word of caring and deep feelings. John encourages the beloved of God to love each other because God is love. You are the beloved of God!

Since God is love, and we are his children, then we need to love each other and walk in love. We can love everyone because we have experienced the love of God for ourselves. In your everyday life, remember to walk in love and love all, even those who are not nice to you. Pray for them, and ask the Lord to help you to walk in love and love them. Most importantly, remember that God loves you.

<u>Say it, Believe it, Think it, and Be It!</u>
I am God's beloved; He loves me!

<u>Write Today's Promise</u>

_____

_____

<u>Write Today's Confession</u>

_____

_____

<u>What Do You Think about Today's Promise?</u>

_____

_____

In Christ I Am...
I Am Liked By God
Matthew 17:1-3

Now after six days Jesus took Peter, James, and John his brother, led them up on a high mountain by themselves; and He was transfigured before them. His face shone like the sun, and His clothes became as white as the light. And behold, Moses and Elijah appeared to them, talking with Him.

The topics of 'love' and 'like' can be sometimes hard to explain. I think it is fair to say that we all want to be liked. We want to hang around our friends that we like and who like us.. We know that God loves us, but do you know if God 'likes' you? The above mentioned verse talks about how Jesus took three of His disciples up to what is called the Mount of Transfiguration. Their names were Peter, James and John. Some believe that they were Jesus' favorite disciples. Others refer to them as Jesus' inner circle. It is clear that Jesus liked Peter, James and John, because he loved spending time with them. In the same way, God loves it when you take time out of your day to spend some time with Him. That is one way of showing him that you love him, but also that you like Him. Better still, I want you to know that God likes you. He likes to spend time with you, and he likes it when you sing songs to Him. He likes it when you pray to him and read his love letter to you. As you go about your everyday life, keep this phrase in mind: God likes me!

<u>Say it, Believe it, Think it, and Be It!</u>
I am liked by God!

<u>Write Today's Promise</u>

_____

_____

<u>Write Today's Confession</u>

_____

_____

<u>What Do You Think about Today's Promise?</u>

_____

_____

Janice Hylton-Thompson

I Am Prayed for

Ephesians 3:14-19

For this reason I bow my knees to the Father of our Lord Jesus Christ, from whom the whole family in heaven and earth is named, that He would grant you, according to the riches of His glory, to be strengthened with might through His Spirit in the inner man.

That Christ may dwell in your hearts through faith; that you, being rooted and grounded in love, may be able to comprehend with all the saints what is the width and length and depth and height—to know the love of Christ which passes knowledge; that you may be filled with all the fullness of God.

Isn't it a blessing when someone prays for you? Paul prayed so that:

1. You may be strengthened with might;
2. Christ may dwell in your hearts through faith;
3. You may be able to comprehend with all the saints what are the width and length and depth and height;
4. You may know the love of Christ which passes knowledge; and
5. You may be filled with all the fullness of God.

<u>Say it, Believe it, Think it, and Be It!</u>
I am saved by grace through faith in Jesus Christ.

<u>Write Today's Promise</u>

_____

_____

<u>Write Today's Confession</u>

_____

_____

<u>What Do You Think about Today's Promise?</u>

_____

_____

In Christ I Am...

I Am Provided for by God

Philippians 4:19

And my God shall supply all your need according to His riches in glory by Christ Jesus.

God your Father promised that He would supply your every need. With this in mind, it does not matter what the need is because God your Father wants you to come to Him with all of your needs. Don't be afraid to ask Him whenever you need food, shelter, clothing, godly friends, healing, or anything else, no matter how large or small it seems, God promised that he would provide all of your needs. Some of your needs are provided through your parents, guardians, and families, but some can only be met by God. There might be times that you need His peace, encouragement, hope and comfort. Whatever the need is, God your Father is ready and able to meet your every need. You only need to ask in faith, believe and then receive the answer in the name of Jesus!

There might be some of you reading this book whose parents might not be able to provide the basic needs. Guess what? You can pray to your Heavenly Father and He will make a way. He will provide for you and supply your needs. Remember that you can go to God your Father about any and every need.

Say it, Believe it, Think it, and Be It!
I am provided for by God my Father!

Write Today's Promise

_____

_____

Write Today's Confession

_____

_____

What Do You Think about Today's Promise?

_____

_____

Janice Hylton-Thompson
I Am Blessed With Everything I Need

Ephesians 1:3

Blessed be the God and Father of our Lord Jesus Christ, who has blessed us with every spiritual blessing in the heavenly places in Christ...

Paul begins this verse with praise to God, the father of our Lord Jesus Christ. Jesus Christ has blessed us with all spiritual blessings in heavenly places. All of the blessings and promises in the Bible were not just for the people alive back then, but they are for you today also.

It is by faith that we believe we have received all the spiritual blessings that God has for us. Some of these blessings are things God has already given us. They are up in the spiritual realm and they are yours. What are spiritual blessings? They are the gifts that come with salvation and faith in Christ such as salvation, peace, healing, speaking in tongues, and more. Receive all of the blessings that God has for you today by your faith in Jesus Christ.

<u>Say it, Believe it, Think it, and Be It!</u>
I am a saint, and I am faithful.

<u>Write Today's Promise</u>

_____
_____

<u>Write Today's Confession</u>

_____
_____

<u>What Do You Think about Today's Promise?</u>

_____
_____

Love Confession

God loves me! I am created for Him and I am chosen for Him. I am chosen in Christ because I am wonderfully made, which makes me the apple of God's eye.

I am taught of the Lord; therefore, I am filled with the fullness of the Lord. I am accepted among the beloved because I am loved by God, and I am His beloved!

God likes me; I am prayed for and provided for. I am blessed with everything I need!

BENEFITS

1 John 2:12

I write to you, little children, because your sins are forgiven you for His name's sake.

John 1:12

But as many as received Him, to them He gave the right to become children of God, to those who believe in His name.

1 Corinthians 5:17

Therefore, if anyone is in Christ, he is a new creation; old things have passed away; behold, all things have become new.

Galatians 3:26

For you are all sons of God through faith in Christ Jesus.

1 John 5:14-15

Now this is the confidence that we have in Him, that if we ask anything according to His will, He hears us. And if we know that He hears us, whatever we ask, we know that we have the petitions that we have asked of Him.

In Christ I Am...
I Am Heard by God
1 John 5:14-15

Now this is the confidence that we have in Him, that if we ask anything according to His will, He hears us. And if we know that He hears us, whatever we ask, we know that we have the petitions that we have asked of Him.

This is one of my favorite scriptures! 'Prayer' is another one of those words in the Bible that some struggle with. 'To pray' simply means to communicate with God. It's that easy! If you want to be more specific, prayer is talking to God about what He has said to you in His Word. This is why it is important to spend time with the Lord by reading and meditating or thinking on His word. This book is a perfect tool to help you get to know God more in His Word.

In this verse, John says that we have this confidence or trust in God, that if we ask anything according to His will, which is His Word, then we know that He hears us. And since we know that He hears us, we know that we have those things that we asked of Him. I encourage you to spend time in God's Word. As you do, your confidence in Him and His Word will grow. When you pray, you can trust and know that God has heard you and that you have those things that you have prayed for.

<u>Say it, Believe it, Think it, and Be It!</u>
God hears me every time I pray because I pray according to his will.

<u>Write Today's Promise</u>

_____

_____

<u>Write Today's Confession</u>

_____

_____

<u>What Do You Think about Today's Promise?</u>

_____

_____

I Am Destined

Ephesians 1:5

Having predestined us to adoption as sons by Jesus Christ to Himself, according to the good pleasure of His will.

We will look at two important words today. The first is 'predestined' which means that you were chosen ahead of time by God to be His child. The second is 'adoption', which means to take a child that is not biologically yours as your own, and to become that child's legal parent. So when we combine these two important and powerful words, we get the following — God chose you before He created the earth to become His child!

You were destined by God before He thought about creating the earth to be His child. This is very powerful and encouraging. God wants you! God loves you! God chose you! Among everyone else in this world, God has chosen you because He loves you.

<u>Say it, Believe it, Think it, and Be It!</u>

God chose me ahead of time to be his child. I am destined by God

<u>Write Today's Promise</u>

_____

_____

<u>Write Today's Confession</u>

_____

_____

<u>What Do You Think about Today's Promise?</u>

_____

_____

In Christ I Am...

I Am Kept By God

Jude 1:24-25

Now to Him who is able to keep you from stumbling, and to present you faultless before the presence of His glory with exceeding joy. To God our Savior, Who alone is wise, be glory and majesty, Dominion and power, both now and forever. Amen.

Let's focus on verse 24 for today. In this portion of scripture Jude, the brother of our Lord Jesus Christ, gives a benediction. A benediction is a final blessing which is given at the end of Christian services. Jude wants you to be assured that God your Father is able to keep you from stumbling and to present you faultless before the Lord with exceeding joy. Notice how the verse said that God will keep you from stumbling and he will present you faultless. In your everyday walk with the Lord, depend on Christ to keep you by submitting totally to Him. Even though you sin, if you trust Christ for your salvation, you can have confidence that He will find you faultless.

Remember: it is not about you and how good you are, but it is about Christ dying on the cross. God is able to keep you from making mistakes, to protect you, and to provide for your every need. Whatever you need, know that God is able to do it, and because of Christ, God has already done everything for you.

Say it, Believe it, Think it, and Be It!

I am kept by God, and he presents me faultless.

Write Today's Promise

_____

_____

Write Today's Confession

_____

_____

What Do You Think about Today's Promise?

_____

_____

Janice Hylton-Thompson

I Am Planted in God

Psalm 1:3

He shall be like a tree planted by the rivers of water that brings forth its fruit in its season, whose leaf also shall not wither; and whatever he does shall prosper.

The word 'tree' is used here to represent a person, and specifically it represents how you are to be in God. Trees may sway a little in the breeze, but when they have firm roots in place, they have nothing to fear from strong winds or loud storms. When you read and meditate on God's Word instead of what people say and think, you will be like this tree. You will be able to firmly stand on the promises of God and only believe his Word of God. You will feed on God's goodness, grace, love, and mercy. Choose to be the tree that will keep standing, no matter what comes or goes.

Say it, Believe it, Think it, and Be It!
I am planted by the rivers of water.

Write Today's Promise
_____
_____

Write Today's Confession
_____
_____

What Do You Think about Today's Promise?
_____
_____

In Christ I Am...

I Am Favored

Proverbs 21:1

The king's heart is in the hand of the Lord, like the rivers of water; He turns it wherever He wishes.

God, your Heavenly Father, has many good promises for you because He loves you so much. The Lord's will for you is that you find favor with everyone you come in contact with. The Lord will turn the hearts of those that you need to have favor with toward you so that you can have what you need to have.

God's hand is involved in your life in every way and for everything. This book is important because it teaches you the promises of God and how He desires for them to be fulfilled in your life. As you go about your daily walk, remember that God favors you! Going to school, confess that you are favored. While you take an exam, confess that you are favored. When you are around your friends, confess that you are favored.

<u>Say it, Believe it, Think it, and Be It!</u>
I am favored by God in every area of my life.

<u>Write Today's Promise</u>

_____

_____

<u>Write Today's Confession</u>

_____

_____

<u>What Do You Think about Today's Promise?</u>

_____

_____

Janice Hylton-Thompson

I Am Protected

Psalm 34:7

The angel of the Lord encamps all around those who fear Him, and delivers them.

Did you know that God has angels watching over you? This verse specifically states that it is the angel of the Lord who encamps around, or protects, those who fear the Lord. Here, the word 'fear' does not mean 'to be afraid,' but it means 'to revere or respect.' How do you fear the Lord? Well, you have already taken the first step by inviting Jesus Christ into your heart. You revere and respect the Lord our God by being obedient to Him and His Word. Notice the verse said 'all around'? Not only does God protect you physically, but I believe that he also protects your heart, mind, and soul, which consists of your will, intellect, and emotions. When you pray, believe that God has surrounded you in every area of your life. Do not allow the enemy to have any influence over any part of you; confess instead that the angel of the Lord has encamped around you.

Say it, Believe it, Think it, and Be It!

I am protected by God because the angel of the Lord surrounds me.

Write Today's Promise

_____
_____

Write Today's Confession

_____
_____

What Do You Think about Today's Promise?

_____
_____

In Christ I Am...

I Am Healthy

3 John 2:2

Beloved, I pray that you may prosper in all things and be in health, just as your soul prospers.

We looked at this verse earlier in the area of being financially blessed. Now, I want us to look at it in the area of health. The Apostle John says that not only does your Heavenly Father want you and your family to be blessed financially and be prosperous in every area of your life, but He also wants you to be prosperous in your body.

Christ died and took every sickness and disease upon and within Him so that you can be healthy. This does not just mean physically healthy, but also emotionally, psychologically and mentally. Christ became poor so that you can become rich. Christ's desire is that you are blessed in your body, home, finances, and family. Notice that John ended this verse by saying 'as your soul prospers.' Your soul prospering began when you first accepted Jesus. Now, it continues to prosper as you learn of Jesus and His Word. As you read and study the Bible and learn of Jesus, your soul will prosper, and you will find your will being strengthened and your intellect and emotions being sharpened.

<u>Say it, Believe it, Think it, and Be It!</u>
I am healthy in every area of my body.

<u>Write Today's Promise</u>

_____

_____

<u>Write Today's Confession</u>

_____

_____

<u>What Do You Think about Today's Promise?</u>

_____

_____

Janice Hylton-Thompson

I Am an Overcomer

Revelation 12:11

And they overcame him by the blood of the Lamb and by the word of their testimony, and they did not love their lives to the death.

The Apostle John, known as the disciple whom Jesus loved, is the author of the book of Revelation. Today's verse lists two very powerful weapons that can help you live a victorious Christian life. The first weapon is 'the blood' of Jesus Christ. You have overcome or won against the enemy because of the blood of Christ. Plead or say "the blood of Jesus covers me!" Thank God that because of the blood of Jesus Christ, you are healed, forgiven and protected. Because of the blood of Jesus, no weapon that the enemy forms against you shall prosper.

The second weapon is the 'Word of God.' It is very important to know God's Word. You learn God's Word by reading the Bible, by reading books like this one, by going to Sunday school or youth church, by going to youth conferences, and many other ways. You are already an overcomer. The enemy will accuse you of mistakes that you make, but remember that all of your sins have been paid for by Christ and that you are an overcomer. That means you're a winner!

<u>Say it, Believe it, Think it, and Be It!</u>
I am an overcomer by the blood of Jesus Christ.

<u>Write Today's Promise</u>

_____

_____

<u>Write Today's Confession</u>

_____

_____

<u>What Do You Think about Today's Promise?</u>

_____

_____

In Christ I Am...

I Am Wise

Proverbs 23:24

*The father of the righteous will greatly rejoice,
and he who begets a wise child will delight in him.*

To be 'righteous' means to be in right standing with God! You are righteous because of the blood of the Lord Jesus. You are righteous and your parents will rejoice because you are righteous. The verse goes on to say that the parent who gives birth to a wise child will be happy. King Solomon was the wisest person who ever lived next to the Lord Jesus Christ.

The important thing to know about King Solomon is that he asked God for wisdom. Throughout the scriptures, you will find a number of verses on wisdom. Wisdom is so important that if you don't have it, God wants you to ask Him for it. Asking for wisdom from God is like asking Him for anything else. Go ahead and ask the Lord to bless you with wisdom and to help you to be a wise person in all that you do.

<u>Say it, Believe it, Think it, and Be It!</u>
I am righteous and wise, and I make my parents happy!

<u>Write Today's Promise</u>

_____

_____

<u>Write Today's Confession</u>

_____

_____

<u>What Do You Think about Today's Promise?</u>

_____

_____

Janice Hylton-Thompson

I Am Victorious

1 Corinthians 15:57

But thanks be to God, who gives us the victory through
our Lord Jesus Christ.

It is important to understand that everything that you have is because of Jesus Christ. Because of Him, you are saved, filled with the Holy Spirit, blessed, and protected. Because of Him, you are victorious. It is God's will for you to be victorious and have the victory in every situation. No matter what situation you face, whether you are in school, at home, with your friends, or with those who do not like you, keep in mind that you are victorious, and God has already made you a winner. When you have a test in school, remember that you are victorious. If you are sick in your body, remember that because of Jesus Christ, you are victorious in your healing. Jesus died so that you could be healed. You may not always feel victorious – but that's when it's the most important to remember God's truth!

<u>Say it, Believe it, Think it, and Be It!</u>
I am victorious through Jesus Christ.

<u>Write Today's Promise</u>

_____

_____

<u>Write Today's Confession</u>

_____

_____

<u>What Do You Think about Today's Promise?</u>

_____

_____

Benefits Confession

I am heard by God and I am destined. God keeps me, and I am planted in Him.

I am favored, protected, and healthy! I am an overcomer, I am wise, and I am victorious!

Janice Hylton-Thompson

EMPOWERED

Acts 1:8

But you shall receive power when the Holy Spirit has come upon you; and you shall be witnesses to Me in Jerusalem, and in all Judea and Samaria, and to the end of the earth.

Philippians 4:13

I can do all things through Christ who strengthens me.

Proverbs 18:21

The king's heart is in the hand of the Lord, Like the rivers of water; He turns it wherever He wishes.

In Christ I Am...
I Am Called by God To Walk Worthy

Ephesians 4:1

I, therefore, the prisoner of the Lord, beseech you to walk worthy of the calling with which you were called.

Paul, the apostle of the Lord, was often jailed because of his love for the Lord. In this verse, he encourages the body of believers to walk worthy of the calling which we have been called, which is to be like Jesus. When he says 'walk,' he's talking about a consistent and ongoing relationship between us and Jesus. Every day in your walk and with your words, be Christ-like; try to think and act more like Christ.

Each day, as you go through your daily routine, think about what Jesus has done for you. Think of the price He paid for your freedom from sins. Walk worthy of the Lord and His love because you have been called to be a representative of the Lord Jesus Christ.

<u>Say it, Believe it, Think it, and Be It!</u>
I am walking worthy of the calling that I have been called to be Christ-like.

<u>Write Today's Promise</u>

_____

_____

<u>Write Today's Confession</u>

_____

_____

<u>What Do You Think about Today's Promise?</u>

_____

_____

Janice Hylton-Thompson

I Am Growing in Christ

Colossians 2:6-7

As you therefore have received Christ Jesus the Lord, so walk in Him, rooted and built up in Him and established in the faith, as you have been taught, abounding in it with thanksgiving.

Walking in Christ can also be described as growing in Christ. So, as you have received Christ Jesus, walk in Him! The word 'abounding' means God wants you to be firmly planted in Him. If you are rooted, then you are established like a firmly planted and growing tree. It does not matter what comes or goes; you will continue to be rooted in Christ. To be built up in Him means to continually grow in Christ. Every day, you are building upon what you learned yesterday, and adding to what you will learn tomorrow. Don't be upset with yourself simply because you're not perfect yet. God is still working on you!

You are also established in faith. Think of your forefathers and foremothers in the Bible, who have walked the path of faith. Think of those youth in the Bible who lived for God, no matter what the circumstances were.

<u>Say it, Believe it, Think it, and Be It!</u>
I am growing in Christ every day.

<u>Write Today's Promise</u>

_____

_____

<u>Write Today's Confession</u>

_____

_____

<u>What Do You Think about Today's Promise?</u>

_____

_____

In Christ I Am...

I Am Humble

1 Peter 5:6

Therefore humble yourselves under the mighty hand of God, that He may exalt you in due time.

The word 'humble' or 'humility' is another one of those words that can be difficult to define, understand and apply. It has been taught that humility is to think negatively, or to think lowly about ourselves. Instead of saying, "I am the righteousness of Christ," some feel that to be humble means to say "I am dirty and filthy." This, however, is far from the truth. To humble ourselves is to receive and accept the teaching of the Lord while allowing it to change us, and so we become more like Christ. Submit yourself to God, listen to him, obey him, and do as he teaches in the Bible. Do not boast, but instead, only speak what God has said. Another thing I would like to point out is that you will hear people pray and say, "Lord, humble me." The scriptures, however, invites us to humble ourselves under God's mighty hand, and in due time he will exalt us. Some feel that when bad things happen to us, that is God's way of humbling us. According to the verse above, this thinking is incorrect. We are to humble ourselves by allowing God's word to teach us as we submit ourselves to God's word. Don't ever call yourself dirty, imperfect, or worthless. You are beloved by God!

<u>Say it, Believe it, Think it, and Be It!</u>
I humble myself, by submitting to the Lord. I am humble!

<u>Write Today's Promise</u>

_____

_____

<u>Write Today's Confession</u>

_____

_____

<u>What Do You Think about Today's Promise?</u>

_____

_____

Janice Hylton-Thompson

I Am a Worshipper

Jude 1:24-25

Now to Him who is able to keep you from stumbling, and to present you faultless before the presence of His glory with exceeding joy. To God our Savior, Who alone is wise, be glory and majesty, Dominion and power, both now and forever. Amen.

Jude ends his book by praising and worshipping the Lord. He acknowledges that the God of the Bible is God and Savior. He states that God is our savior, and He alone is wise because Christ alone is all-knowing. To the only one that is all-knowing, be glory and majesty, dominion and power, both now and forever!

The above-mentioned words or phrases are used to honor God to let Him know how much we love and adore Him. Only God is worthy of all of your praise and adoration. The beautiful thing is that, like prayer, you can praise and worship God wherever you are. You do not have to wait until you go to Church, but you can praise him while you are taking a shower or eating your breakfast. Go ahead and show God how much you love Him by praising and worshipping Him.

<u>Say it, Believe it, Think it, and Be It!</u>

I am a worshipper, so I worship, praise, honor, and adore you Lord.

<u>Write Today's Promise</u>

_____
_____

<u>Write Today's Confession</u>

_____
_____

<u>What Do You Think about Today's Promise?</u>

_____
_____

In Christ I Am...

I Am Holy as God Is

1 Peter 1:15-16

But as he which hath called you is holy, so be ye holy in all manner of conversation; because it is written, be ye holy; for I am holy.

If someone asked you to define 'holy,' what would you say. Some people think that it has to do with works, while others think that it has to do with women wearing long dresses and not putting a perm in their hair. But, in actuality, being holy has to do with being like God.

You become like Christ by first accepting Jesus Christ as Lord and the Savior of your life. At the point that you accept Christ, God sees you as holy! Then you need to begin to renew your mind by reading and meditating on God's Word. When you read God's Word, allow it to work in your life by changing you. This will result in becoming more and more like Christ. When you allow God's Word to change your heart and renew your mind, you are holy. When you think like Christ and talk like him, you are holy. As you read and study these scriptures in this book and become more like Christ, you are holy.

<u>Say it, Believe it, Think it, and Be It!</u>
I am holy in all areas of my life

<u>Write Today's Promise</u>

_____
_____

<u>Write Today's Confession</u>

_____
_____

<u>What Do You Think about Today's Promise?</u>

_____
_____

Janice Hylton-Thompson

I Am Christ's Helper

2 Corinthians 6:1

We then, as workers together with Him also plead with you not to receive the grace of God in vain.

There is a difference between the law of the Old Testament and the grace of the New Testament. When Christ died, the law was fulfilled, and we now live by the grace of God through faith. Remember earlier when we talked about what it meant to be saved? We discussed how we are saved by having faith that Jesus Christ died for you so you can become one with Him. Now that you are one with Christ, you are to be His helper and share His love with others. God's grace was not given to you in vain, but for you to allow it to change your life. By changing your life and sharing God's love and grace with others, you show that you are not taking God's grace in vain. Every time you change and become more like Christ, you show God that His grace toward you is being received and appreciated.

<u>Say it, Believe it, Think it, and Be It!</u>
I am Christ helper! I share the love of Christ with others.

<u>Write Today's Promise</u>

_____

_____

<u>Write Today's Confession</u>

_____

_____

<u>What Do You Think about Today's Promise?</u>

_____

_____

In Christ I Am...
I Am Prosperous
3 John 2:2

Beloved, I pray that you may prosper in all things and be in health, just as your soul prospers.

We used the word 'beloved' earlier in one of our studies. Again, 'beloved' means to be loved of God. You are God's child, and He is concerned with not only your spiritual life but also your natural life. God loves you, so He wants you to prosper or be successful in every area of your life. God your Father wants you to be blessed at home, school, play, and everywhere you go. If it is important to you, then it is important to God.

God wants you to be prosperous in all things, including your health, peace, finances, peace of mind, and everything else you undertake. God wants you and your parents to be blessed, which will result in you being blessed. God wants you and your family to have more than enough so that you can be a blessing to others.

<u>Say it, Believe it, Think it, and Be It!</u>
I prosper in every area of my life.

<u>Write Today's Promise</u>

_____
_____

<u>Write Today's Confession</u>

_____
_____

<u>What Do You Think about Today's Promise?</u>

_____
_____

Janice Hylton-Thompson
I Am Rich-Blessed to be A Blessing!

Proverbs 10:22

**The blessing of the Lord makes one rich,
He adds no sorrow with it.**

Did you know that it scares some people to say that the body of Christ should be rich? In spite of this, God wants you to be rich. Think about it! What does it mean to be poor? What does it mean to be rich? When a family is poor, they do not have enough to take care of themselves. And since they do not have enough to take care of themselves, then they will not have enough to help other families. But if a family is rich or has more than enough, then that family can take care of themselves and then help other families.

They do not have to have millions of dollars, but can give out of what they have. God wants you and your family to be rich. The above verse says that the blessings of the Lord make you and your family rich, not so that you can enjoy a selfish lifestyle of spending money on yourself, but so that you can use your money for Him. He wants you to have more than enough so that you can give to the church and help other families come to know the Lord Jesus Christ. If you keep this in mind, you and your family will always do the right thing when it comes to having money.

Say it, Believe it, Think it, and Be It!

I am rich; my family and I have more than enough so that we can be a blessing to other families.

Write Today's Promise

_____

_____

Write Today's Confession

_____

_____

What Do You Think about Today's Promise?

_____

_____

In Christ I Am...

I Am a Giver

Luke 6:38

Give, and it will be given to you: good measure, pressed down, shaken together, and running over will be put into your bosom. For with the same measure that you use, it will be measured back to you."

Yesterday, we talked about how God has made you and your family blessed so that you can be a blessing to other families. Today, we will see that Jesus has encouraged us to give. Do you remember how we talked about the poor family and the rich family? The poor family did not have enough to take care of themselves, so they would not have enough to give.

We also talked about how being blessed does not have to mean that your family has millions of dollars. When you have more than enough for you and your family and you are able to give to another family, you are blessed. In this verse, Jesus said for us to give, and when we give, it will come back to us. This is why it is important for you to understand that when God blesses you and your family, it is not just for you but for you to share with others.

Say it, Believe it, Think it, and Be It!
I am blessed to be a blessing and I am a giver!

Write Today's Promise

_____

_____

Write Today's Confession

_____

_____

What Do You Think about Today's Promise?

_____

_____

Janice Hylton-Thompson

I Am a Doer of God's Word

James 1:22

But be doers of the word, and not hearers only, deceiving yourselves.

Knowing the Word of God is important because the Word of God is to the spirit what food is to the body. In the same way the food you eat is needed to help you grow up healthy and strong, so is the Word of God needed to help you to grow up in the Lord healthy and strong. This food is needed to help you to grow up in Christ and be mature in Him. When you read, study, and think on God's Word, it brings changes into your life. When you hide God's Word in your heart, it will come out of your mouth in the time that you need it. Not only is it important to know God's Word, but it is just as important to put it into practice. When you read about things to do in the Bible, such as the different topics you are studying in this book, please make them a part of your daily life. They will help you in your walk with the Lord Jesus.

Say it, Believe it, Think it, and Be It!

I am a doer of God's word.

Write Today's Promise

_____

_____

Write Today's Confession

_____

_____

What Do You Think about Today's Promise?

_____

_____

In Christ I Am...

I Am Salt and Light

Matthew 5: 13A & 14A

You are the salt of the earth...
You are the light of the world.

From these two verses, I pulled out the parts that tell you who you are. Think about salt. What does it do? It gives taste to your food. Now, think of light. What does it do? When you walk into a room that is dark, you reach for the light so that you can see. Well, that is who you are! You are salt and light. Bring Jesus to those who don't know Him. In school, you are the light that everyone will draw to. Let your light of Christ shine brightly for everyone to see.

Say it, Believe it, Think it, and Be It!

I am salt to the world, and I am the light of the world. I shine with Christ.

Write Today's Promise

_____

_____

Write Today's Confession

_____

_____

What Do You Think about Today's Promise?

_____

_____

Janice Hylton-Thompson

I Am God's Mouthpiece

Psalm 66:8

**Oh, bless our God, you peoples!
And make the voice of His praise to be heard.**

This is an awesome verse because it is encouraging you to make the voice of God be heard in your praise. This means your mouth is to be used to glorify and praise the Lord and to speak good things. Do not use your mouth to swear, curse, lie, or speak negativity. Be careful of the songs that you sing, because if you listen to the words of some of those songs carefully, there are a lot of curses, sexuality, and negativity in them. You can't use your mouth to swear and say vile things, then turn around and use the same mouth to declare God's blessings over your life. Remember, your enemy the devil is out to kill, steal, and destroy. He will try and trick you into singing words of negativity, and he will try and tell you that they're only words and they're not hurting anybody. Yet if the words of God bring life to every part of you, doesn't it make sense that the words of the devil would bring death? Many of your friends will not see it this way, and may even make fun of you for not singing the songs they sing, but guard your mouth, and use it only for praise.

Say it, Believe it, Think it, and Be It!

I am called to use my mouth for God. I will be careful of what I say and the songs I sing. I will not curse, tell lies, or use profanity.

Write Today's Promise

_____

_____

Write Today's Confession

_____

_____

What Do You Think about Today's Promise?

_____

_____

In Christ I Am...

I Am More than a Conqueror

Romans 8:37

Yet in all these things we are more than conquerors through Him who loved us.

In this life and your walk with the Lord, you will face a lot of trials and tribulations. As you grow in your walk with the Lord, you will sometimes make mistakes and miss the mark. Regardless of these mistakes, remember that Christ has already paid the price for your sins and your mistakes. Do not allow anyone to make you feel guilty of your mistakes. In Christ Jesus, you are more than a conqueror because of Jesus' sacrificial death. No matter what you go through in your life, remember always that God loves you very much with an everlasting love, and He will love you forever.

<u>Say it, Believe it, Think it, and Be It!</u>

I am more than a conqueror in all things through Jesus Christ!

<u>Write Today's Promise</u>

_____

_____

<u>Write Today's Confession</u>

_____

_____

<u>What Do You Think about Today's Promise?</u>

_____

_____

Empowered Confession

I am called by God to walk worthy of the call with which I have been called. Therefore, I am growing in Him, I am humble, I am a worshipper and I am holy as God is.

I am Christ's helper. I am prosperous, rich, and blessed to be a blessing.

I am a giver, a doer of God's word. I am salt and light, God's mouthpiece, and I am more than a conqueror.

What's Next?

Thank you so much for reading my book. I hope that you have enjoyed reading it as much as I have enjoyed writing and reading it over and over again.

I pray that you have learned who you are now that you are in Christ, and I hope that you will apply what you have learned here to your life daily.

If you would like to learn more about who you are in Christ, I encourage you to continue to read the Bible and glean from the truths that are written here.

Additionally, each of these verse can be studied 'topically.' Take the topic of healing for example and study as many verses as possible on it. This will help you to learn more and broaden your knowledge and understanding of the topic of healing.

Sincerely Yours
Janice

About the Author

Janice came to the knowledge of Christ when she was twelve years old, and was born again by confessing Jesus Christ as Lord.

When Janice was eighteen years old, she accepted the call of the Lord Jesus Christ upon her life to be a teacher in the Kingdom of God.

Janice has been anointed and appointed by God for such a time as this, to spread the love of Christ and teach the simplicity of the scriptures all over the earth.

Janice is a much sought-after Bible teacher, author, conference speaker, and workshop facilitator.

Janice is described as an anointed and dynamic young woman, whom God has raised up in the last days to teach the Word of the Lord in simplicity.

Her slogan is: "Teaching God's Word in simplicity, that even a child will understand!"

Janice is known for her simple yet profound, humorous, personal, and practical approach to teaching the scriptures. A prolific and profound orator who is anointed to bring the word of God to life, Janice teaches how to take the Word of God, apply it to one's life and make it personal.

Janice's ministry is under the leadership and covering of her spiritual father

Bishop Marvin Bradshaw Sr.

A graduate of Essex County College and Rutgers State University, Janice resides in Newark, New Jersey with her husband Michael and their children Alexia and Michael Jr.

To Contact The Author:

Please include your testimony or help received from this book when you contact the author.

Your prayer requests are welcome!

For Speaking engagements, Book Signing Events or information, you may contact the author at: (973)573-4381

Or

Janice Hylton Ministries

P.O. Box 9881

Newark NJ 07104

Or

www.janicehylton.org

Or

Facebook

Janice Hylton Ministries

Author Janice Hylton-Thompson

Or

Twitter

@Thejanicehylton

Or

Email

Janice@jhmin.org

Other Books By
Janice Hylton-Thompson

Praying For Our Children

In Christ I Am... Bible Verse Journal

In Christ I Am... Prayer Journal

Please Visit Janice's Ministry Website for a number of other products @
www.janicehylton.org

Credits

A great big thank you and many blessings to everyone who has helped me to bring this book series to life. I could not have done it without you guys. Thanks a million!!

All editors and formatters are also authors themselves. Please visit their websites for further information.

Edited & Proofread by

Jim and Andrea Barringer

http://barringerbooks.com/

http://www.facebook.com/barringerbooks

Developmental Editors

Kelly Hartigan

http://editing.xterraweb.com/

Neil D'Silva

http://www.NeilDSilva.com/

Formatted By

Raymond Clarke

http://raymondclarkeauthor.wordpress.com/

http://www.facebook.com/RClarkeAuthor/

Cover Design by

Ihor Tureh

www.ingramcontent.com/pod-product-compliance
Lightning Source LLC
Chambersburg PA
CBHW051808040426
42446CB00007B/568